THE KEY

STUDENT STUDY GUIDE

Social Studies 20–1

THE KEY student study guide is designed to help students achieve success in school. The content in each study guide is 100% aligned to the provincial curriculum and serves as an excellent source of material for review and practice. To create this book, teachers, curriculum specialists, and assessment experts have worked closely to develop the instructional pieces that explain each of the key concepts for the course. The practice questions and sample tests have detailed solutions that show problem-solving methods, highlight concepts that are likely to be tested, and point out potential sources of errors. ***THE KEY*** is a complete guide to be used by students throughout the school year for reviewing and understanding course content, and to prepare for assessments.

Publisher
Gautam Rao

Contributors
Brigitta Braden
Heather Friedenthal

Rao, Gautam, 1961 –
THE KEY – Social Studies 20-1

1. Social Studies – Juvenile Literature. I. Title:

ISBN: 978-1-77044-422-5
Published by
Castle Rock Research Corp.
2410 Manulife Place
10180 – 101 Street
Edmonton, AB T5J 3S4

10 9 8 7 6 5

Dedicated to the memory of Dr. V. S. Rao

THE KEY – SOCIAL STUDIES 20-1

THE KEY consists of the following sections:

KEY Tips for Being Successful at School gives examples of study and review strategies. It includes information about learning styles, study schedules, and note taking for test preparation.

Class Focus includes a unit on each area of the curriculum. Units are divided into sections, each focusing on one of the specific expectations, or main ideas, that students must learn about in that unit. Examples, definitions, and visuals help to explain each main idea. Practice questions on the main ideas are also included. At the end of each unit is a test on the important ideas covered. The practice questions and unit tests help students identify areas they know and those they need to study more. They can also be used as preparation for tests and quizzes. Each unit is prefaced by a ***Table of Correlations***, which correlates questions in the unit (and in the practice tests at the end of the book) to the specific curriculum expectations. Answers and solutions are found at the end of each unit.

KEY Strategies for Success on Tests helps students get ready for tests. It shows students different types of questions they might see, word clues to look for when reading them, and hints for answering them.

Practice Tests includes one to three tests based on the entire course. They are very similar to the format and level of difficulty that students may encounter on final tests. In some regions, these tests may be reprinted versions of official tests, or reflect the same difficulty levels and formats as official versions. This gives students the chance to practice using real-world examples. Answers and complete solutions are provided at the end of the section.

For the complete curriculum document (including specific expectations along with examples and sample problems), visit http://education.alberta.ca/teachers/core.aspx.

THE KEY *Study Guides* are available for many courses. Check www.castlerockresearch.com for a complete listing of books available for your area.

For information about any of our resources or services, please call Castle Rock Research Corp. at 780.448.9619 or visit our website at http://www.castlerockresearch.com.

At Castle Rock Research, we strive to produce an error-free resource. If you should find an error, please contact us so that future editions can be corrected.

TABLE OF CONTENTS

KEY Tips for Being Successful at School

KEY TIPS FOR BEING SUCCESSFUL AT SCHOOL

KEY FACTORS CONTRIBUTING TO SCHOOL SUCCESS

In addition to learning the content of your courses, there are some other things that you can do to help you do your best at school. You can try some of the following strategies:

- **Keep a positive attitude**: Always reflect on what you can already do and what you already know.
- **Be prepared to learn**: Have the necessary pencils, pens, notebooks, and other required materials for participating in class ready.
- **Complete all of your assignments**: Do your best to finish all of your assignments. Even if you know the material well, practice will reinforce your knowledge. If an assignment or question is difficult for you, work through it as far as you can so that your teacher can see exactly where you are having difficulty.
- **Set small goals for yourself when you are learning new material**: For example, when learning the parts of speech, do not try to learn everything in one night. Work on only one part or section each study session. When you have memorized one particular part of speech and understand it, move on to another one. Continue this process until you have memorized and learned all the parts of speech.
- **Review your classroom work regularly at home**: Review to make sure you understand the material you learned in class.
- **Ask your teacher for help**: Your teacher will help you if you do not understand something or if you are having a difficult time completing your assignments.
- **Get plenty of rest and exercise**: Concentrating in class is hard work. It is important to be well-rested and have time to relax and socialize with your friends. This helps you keep a positive attitude about your schoolwork.
- **Eat healthy meals**: A balanced diet keeps you healthy and gives you the energy you need for studying at school and at home.

How to Find Your Learning Style

Every student learns differently. The manner in which you learn best is called your learning style. By knowing your learning style, you can increase your success at school. Most students use a combination of learning styles. Do you know what type of learner you are? Read the following descriptions. Which of these common learning styles do you use most often?

- Do you need to say things out loud? You may learn best by saying, hearing, and seeing words. You are probably really good at memorizing things such as dates, places, names, and facts. You may need to write down the steps in a process, a formula, or the actions that lead up to a significant event, and then say them out loud.
- Do you need to read or see things? You may learn best by looking at and working with pictures. You are probably really good at puzzles, imagining things, and reading maps and charts. You may need to use strategies like mind mapping and webbing to organize your information and study notes.
- Do you need to draw or write things down? You may learn best by touching, moving, and figuring things out using manipulatives. You are probably really good at physical activities and learning through movement. You may need to draw your finger over a diagram to remember it, tap out the steps needed to solve a problem, or feel yourself writing or typing a formula.

SCHEDULING STUDY TIME

You should review your class notes regularly to ensure that you have a clear understanding of all the new material you learned. Reviewing your lessons on a regular basis helps you to learn and remember ideas and concepts. It also reduces the quantity of material that you need to study prior to a test. Establishing a study schedule will help you to make the best use of your time.

- Regardless of the type of study schedule you use, you may want to consider the following suggestions to maximize your study time and effort:
- Organize your work so that you begin with the most challenging material first.
- Divide the subject's content into small, manageable chunks.
- Alternate regularly between your different subjects and types of study activities in order to maintain your interest and motivation.
- Make a daily list with headings like "Must Do," "Should Do," and "Could Do."
- Begin each study session by quickly reviewing what you studied the day before.
- Maintain your usual routine of eating, sleeping, and exercising to help you concentrate better for extended periods of time.

Creating Study Notes

Mind-Mapping or Webbing

Use the key words, ideas, or concepts from your class notes to create a mind map or web, which is a diagram or visual representation of the given information. A mind map or web is sometimes referred to as a knowledge map. Use the following steps to create a mind map or web:

1. Write the key word, concept, theory, or formula in the centre of your page.
2. Write down related facts, ideas, events, and information, and link them to the central concept with lines.
3. Use coloured markers, underlining, or symbols to emphasize things such as relationships, timelines, and important information.

The following mind map is an example of one that could help you develop an essay:

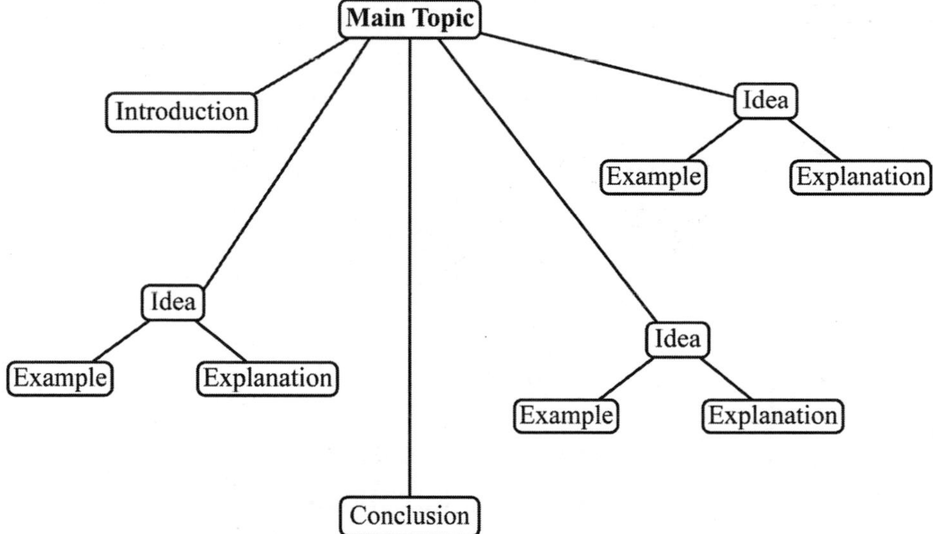

INDEX CARDS

To use index cards while studying, follow these steps:

1. Write a key word or question on one side of an index card.
2. On the reverse side, write the definition of the word, answer to the question, or any other important information that you want to remember.

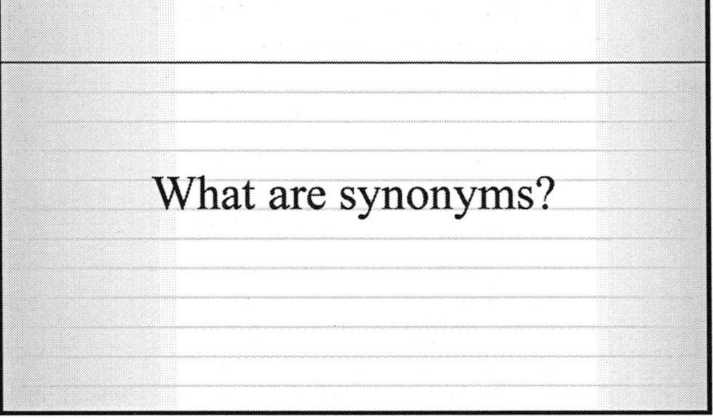

What are synonyms?
Synonyms are words that have the same or almost the same meaning.

For example, "coarse" is a synonym for "rough"

SYMBOLS AND STICKY NOTES—IDENTIFYING IMPORTANT INFORMATION

Use symbols to mark your class notes. For example, an exclamation mark (!) might be used to point out something that must be learned well because it is a very important idea. A question mark (?) may highlight something you are not certain about, and a diamond (◊) or asterisk (*) could highlight interesting information that you want to remember. Sticky notes are useful in the following situations:

- Use sticky notes when you are not allowed to put marks in books.
- Use sticky notes to mark a page in a book that contains an important diagram, formula, explanation, or other information.
- Use sticky notes to mark important facts in research books.

Memorization Techniques

The following techniques can help you when you need to memorize something:

- **Association** relates new learning to something you already know. For example, to remember the spelling difference between dessert and desert, recall that the word *sand* has only one *s*. So, because there is sand in a desert, the word *desert* has only one *s*.
- **Mnemonic** devices are sentences that you create to remember a list or group of items. For example, the first letter of each word in the phrase "**E**very **G**ood **B**oy **D**eserves **F**udge" helps you to remember the names of the lines on the treble-clef staff (E, G, B, D, and F) in music.
- **Acronyms** are words that are formed from the first letters or parts of the words in a group. For example, RADAR is actually an acronym for Radio Detecting and Ranging, and MASH is an acronym for Mobile Army Surgical Hospital. HOMES helps you to remember the names of the five Great Lakes (Huron, Ontario, Michigan, Erie, and Superior).

- **Visualizing** requires you to use your mind's eye to "see" a chart, list, map, diagram, or sentence as it is in your textbook or notes, on the chalkboard or computer screen, or in a display.
- **Initialisms** are abbreviations that are formed from the first letters or parts of the words in a group. Unlike acronyms, an initialism cannot be pronounced as a word itself. For example, BEDMAS is an initialism for the order of operations in math (Brackets, Exponents, Divide, Multiply, Add, Subtract).

KEY Strategies for Reviewing

Reviewing textbook material, class notes, and handouts should be an ongoing activity. Spending time reviewing becomes more critical when you are preparing for a test. You may find some of the following review strategies useful when studying during your scheduled study time:

- Before reading a selection, preview it by noting the headings, charts, graphs, and chapter questions.
- Before reviewing a unit, note the headings, charts, graphs, and chapter questions.
- Highlight key concepts, vocabulary, definitions, and formulas.
- Skim the paragraph, and note the key words, phrases, and information.
- Carefully read over each step in a procedure.
- Draw a picture or diagram to help make the concept clearer.

KEY Strategies for Success: A Checklist

Reviewing is a huge part of doing well at school and preparing for tests. Here is a checklist for you to keep track of how many suggested strategies for success you are using. Read each question, and put a check mark (✓) in the correct column. Look at the questions where you have checked the "No" column. Think about how you might try using some of these strategies to help you do your best at school.

***KEY* Strategies for Success**	**Yes**	**No**
Do you attend school regularly?		
Do you know your personal learning style—how you learn best?		
Do you spend 15 to 30 minutes a day reviewing your notes?		
Do you study in a quiet place at home?		
Do you clearly mark the most important ideas in your study notes?		
Do you use sticky notes to mark texts and research books?		
Do you practise answering multiple-choice and written-response questions?		
Do you ask your teacher for help when you need it?		
Are you maintaining a healthy diet and sleep routine?		
Are you participating in regular physical activity?		

Related Issue 1

RELATED ISSUE 1

Table of Correlations

Specific Outcome	Practice Questions	Unit Test Questions	Practice Test 1	Practice Test 2
Students will explore the relationships among identity, nation and nationalism.				
1.5 explore a range of expressions of nationalism	1, 2	5, 7	1	
1.6 develop understandings of nation and nationalism (relationship to land, geographic, collective, civic, ethnic, cultural, linguistic, political, spiritual, religious, patriotic)	3, 4	1, 6, 9, 13, 14	2, 29, 45, 46	28, 29, 30, 31
1.7 analyze the relationship between nation and nation-state	5, 6	4	48	32
1.8 analyze how the development of nationalism is shaped by historical, geographic, political, economic and social factors (French Revolution and Napoleonic era, contemporary examples)	7, 8	2, 8, 15	30, 31	33, 34
1.9 analyze nationalism as an identity, internalized feeling and/or collective consciousness shared by a people (French Revolution and Napoleonic era, Canadian nationalism, Québécois nationalism, American nationalism, First Nations and Métis nationalism, Inuit perspectives)	9	3, 10		18
1.10 evaluate the importance of reconciling contending nationalist loyalties (Canadian nationalism, First Nations and Métis nationalism, ethnic nationalism in Canada, civic nationalism in Canada, Québécois nationalism, Inuit perspectives on nationalism)	10, 11	11, 17, 19	47, 49	
1.11 evaluate the importance of reconciling nationalism with contending non-nationalist loyalties (religion, region, culture, race, ideology, class, other contending loyalties)	12, 13	12, 16, 18		35

RELATED ISSUE 1

To What Extent Should Nation be the Foundation of Identity?

Identity – In social studies, the term *identity* refers to a condition in which people feel a sense of similarity or sameness with others of their religion, race, ethnicity, or nationality. It is a feeling that can be solidified through symbols thought to represent these similarities, such as the Maple Leaf in Canada or the Star of David for Jewish people. It can also be developed through a shared history, language, or effort to ensure traditions associated with a group are passed through generations.

Nation – The term *nation* refers to a group of people living in or related to a specific geographic region. A nation often has a sovereign government and possesses distinct laws, cultures, and traditions.

Nationalism – A feeling of pride in and devotion to one's country or nation.

Aboriginal – A term encompassing First Nations, Métis, and Inuit peoples.

1.5 explore a range of expressions of nationalism

Expressions of Nationalism

Expressions of nationalism take many different forms. Some tangible examples include flying a national flag or singing a national anthem. Nationalism can be expressed through pride in the military or support for government policies. It can also be expressed through the celebration of holidays, such as Canada Day or Bastille Day in France. Citizens often express feelings of nationalism at international events, such as the Olympics, through support for their country's teams or representatives. Sometimes, people express nationalism by celebrating similarities with others in terms of cultures, languages, or traditions. The desire to protect these similarities is another way of expressing nationalism.

Practice Questions: 1 and 2

1.6 develop understandings of nation and nationalism (relationship to land, geographic, collective, civic, ethnic, cultural, linguistic, political, spiritual, religious, patriotic)

Understanding Nation and Nationalism

There are many different types of nationalism because people in a nation feel different connections to each other and their environment. A person's relationship to the land can create feelings of nationalism. This connection to the environment can be generations old and can cause people to feel a sense of sameness with those around them who share a history with that region. A collective sense of nationalism is when people believe themselves to be part of a group unique to other groups. Shared experiences, language, beliefs, goals, or culture can make people feel like part of a group, thus encouraging a feeling of nationhood.

Civic nationalism binds people together through a shared belief in the same laws, values, and political traditions. It is capable of uniting people who do not share the same race, ethnicity, culture, or language. **Ethnic nationalism** develops when people share a common ethnic history, usually with many generations of ancestors sharing that ethnicity. **Cultural nationalism** develops when a group of people share a common culture with similar traditions, artistic expressions, foods, and attire. Often, people who share a cultural nationalism share the same ethnicity, but this is not always true. **Linguistic nationalism** exists among people who share a similar language and a desire to protect it, even if they are of different ethnicities or cultures. **Political nationalism** exists when people share a desire to govern themselves independently and without influence from other countries. Although people in such a group may not actually have their own country, they share a sense of nationalism out of the desire to achieve this autonomy. **Religious nationalism** exists when people share the same or similar religious beliefs, even if they live in different countries and speak different languages. **Spiritual nationalism** is closely related to both religion and a person's relationship to the land. Religious beliefs may spur feelings of spirituality about a geographic location, which creates a sense of nationhood among people. Sometimes, people will make pilgrimages to these places, which also strengthens their feelings of nationalism and connectedness with the area. **Patriotic nationalism** exists when people have a shared feeling of love for their country. These people may speak different languages or practice different religions, but their common sense of love for their country creates a sense of nationalism among them.

Practice Questions: 3 and 4

1.7 analyze the relationship between nation and nation-state

The Relationship Between Nation and Nation-State

A **nation-state** is a sovereign country in which the majority of its citizens often share common cultures, traditions, and languages. A nation-state has its own system of government, currency, and official language(s). A **nation** can refer to a group of people with similar cultures, traditions, and languages who inhabit a specific area but do not have the ability to govern themselves and who do not possess characteristics of a nation-state (e.g., currency). In some instances, nation-states have been created when the leaders of various nations decide they would like to unite and form an independent country.

Practice Questions: 5 and 6

1.8 analyze how the development of nationalism is shaped by historical, geographic, political, economic and social factors (French Revolution and Napoleonic era, contemporary examples)

The Development of Nationalism

The development of nationalism is shaped by many factors. One such factor is history because people who share a similar history often feel a sense of connection with one another. Geography can help to shape nationalism, as people who have a sense of connection with a region may feel connected to others who live or have lived in that same area. A contemporary example of the influence of both of these factors can be seen in Israel, where Jewish people who share a common history also believe the region in which their country exists to be one that has been given to them by God. Israelis have a strong sense of nationalism partly as a result of these two factors.

Political and economic factors also help develop nationalism as people work together to improve political and/or economic situations within their country. Belief in particular political or economic systems and attempts to implement or retain them can also foster a sense of nationalism. In addition, people with similar political or economic status in a society may feel a sense of sameness with each other that can lead to feelings of nationalism. Social factors are also influential in the development of nationalism. People may join together to improve social situations within a country, which can create feelings of nationalism as they work toward a common goal.

As a result of the French Revolution and the Napoleonic Era, the development of nationalism grew quickly throughout Europe, and old methods of running countries were widely challenged. The French Revolution was fuelled by political, economic, and social factors, as the peasant classes began to demand changes to the ways in which French society was structured. The ruling elite was made up of members of the nobility and members of the Catholic Church, both of whom represented a very small proportion of the population but held many privileges and most of the wealth. The majority of the population was poor, with little or no influence on decisions made concerning their country. Ideas about egalitarianism and liberalism spread as a result of the Enlightenment and were promoted by philosophers, such as Voltaire, who began to suggest that all people were entitled to certain rights regardless of their social standing. People began to demand better living conditions, political influence, and elected governments accountable to the people. In addition, the monarchy had put the country into extreme debt as a result of the spending habits of Louis XVI and his continued support of the American Revolution. As citizens sought change and united in the fight for it, a strong sense of nationalism developed.

The French Revolution gained speed, and historical events such as the Storming of the Bastille in 1789 became a symbol of the potential power of the people if they were united toward a common goal. Although the revolutionaries' goals at first were to limit the king's power and draft a constitution, the revolution went much further than that. By the time the Reign of Terror (1793–94) ended, the king and his wife had been beheaded and the entire structure of French government had disintegrated.

In 1799, the Napoleonic Era began when Napoleon became the leader of France. He immediately introduced some stability to the country. Napoleon furthered the ideas of liberalism and nationalism that had developed during the revolution and spread these ideas throughout Europe. As a result, people in other countries began to demand similar changes. Groups of people who shared similar languages and cultures began to desire national self-determination rather than being controlled by large empires that rarely had the people's best interests in mind. People wanted their own countries to exist on land that had been inhabited by their ancestors for generations, and they wanted autonomy both in terms of politics and culture. Although monarchs attempted to stop the growth of these nationalistic feelings and achieve **legitimacy** (a return to monarch control with little concern for the nationalistic feelings of the citizens), nationalism was a force that was unstoppable and that eventually became a major contributing factor to the First World War. Whether Napoleon was a hero for the rights of the people or a violent dictator is still something that is debated by historians. Today, France is a very nationalistic country, and many of the feelings of nationalism that exist among its citizens are a result of its history. Even the French national anthem "*La Marseillaise*" is based on the events of the French Revolution.

A contemporary example of people's desire to see their nationalistic feelings recognized on a geographic scale was observed during the breakup of Yugoslavia during the 1990s. Several different ethnic groups had inhabited that area for a very long time, and tension developed when some of those groups within Yugoslavia began to demand independence. For example, the Serbians did not want to give up land they believed to be rightfully theirs or to live in areas then controlled by other ethnic groups. Today, the region once known as Yugoslavia is made up of four different countries—Slovenia, Croatia, Bosnia and Herzegovina, and Serbia and Montenegro, although tension still exists within Serbia over the province of Kosovo. Kosovo declared its independence in February of 2008, sparking violence and international debate over the legitimacy of its independence claims.

Another contemporary example of such nationalism is in the country of Israel. Created in 1948 as a homeland for the Jewish people after the atrocities of the Second World War, a great deal of violence has occurred in this area. The primary conflict is between the Israelis and Palestinians, who both lay claim to many parts of the country and have support from various parts of the international community. Several wars have been fought in the area since the creation of Israel, largely as a result of the extreme feelings of nationalism felt by the people who live there.

Practice Questions: 7 and 8

1.9 analyze nationalism as an identity, internalized feeling and/or collective consciousness shared by a people (French Revolution and Napoleonic era, Canadian nationalism, Québécois nationalism, American nationalism, First Nations and Métis nationalism, Inuit perspectives)

Analyzing Nationalism

Feelings of nationalism can be internalized within a group of people so that a collective consciousness toward nationalism exists among a nation's members. People may take the characteristics of the country or nation about which they feel nationalistic and make these characteristics part of their collective identity. The strong beliefs in equality and democracy that developed during the French Revolution and the Napoleonic Era had a strong influence on French nationalism and continue to influence the feelings of French citizens today. Both the French flag and national anthem have their roots in the events and symbols of the Revolution. Pride in a historical figure such as Napoleon and the changes brought to Europe as a result of his policies and actions also influence French nationalism.

Different groups within a country often have very different views of nationalism and identity. For example, the present makeup of the French population has changed drastically as a result of immigration, and many people who live in France today do not share nationalistic pride of people who have long-standing French roots. In the United States, pride and devotion to the country is often considered to be part of being an American. Both historical and contemporary events fuel these feelings. Pride as a result of achieving independence and the current level of influence America has around the world are two such examples. In a common outward display of nationalism, many average American citizens fly the American flag outside their homes. In addition, many people who live in the United States consider themselves Americans first and New Yorkers, Texans, etc., second. American society is very diverse, but most citizens are still proud to call themselves American.

Canada's attitude toward embracing differences and promoting integration rather than assimilation has had an impact on how citizens view Canadian nationalism and identity. Typically, Canadians do not outwardly display nationalistic feelings with as much vigour as Americans. However, because the French culture is in the minority in Canada, the Francophone population in Canada often feels it is essential that their culture be distinct from the rest of Canada in order to preserve it. Québécois nationalism has been a force in Canada for decades as the French population struggles to maintain its place in Canada despite many challenges. Feelings of Québécois nationalism are often internalized within the Québécois population, and it is part of their identity.

First Nations and Métis nationalism has increased in the past few decades, and along with it, demands for political parity, treaty settlements, and compensation for past wrongs against Aboriginal peoples have also increased. In addition, recognition of the roles played by First Nations and Métis peoples in the development of Canada is growing. First Nations and Métis people have worked hard to overcome attempts at assimilation and to instill pride and interest in their culture and history among their youth as well as among people who are not First Nations or Métis. As First Nations people have worked together to address issues from the past, a stronger sense of nationalism has developed among them. Although the Inuit do not face the same issues in terms of reconciling differences and conflicts over treaties, maintenance of their culture and preservation of traditional ways of life are issues that threaten Inuit nationalism.

Practice Question: 9

1.10 evaluate the importance of reconciling contending nationalist loyalties (Canadian nationalism, First Nations and Métis nationalism, ethnic nationalism in Canada, civic nationalism in Canada, Québécois nationalism, Inuit perspectives on nationalism)

Contending Nationalistic Loyalties

Sometimes, a person's feelings of nationalism for the country he or she lives in may conflict with feelings of nationalism he or she has for another country or nation. This is not uncommon among people who have come to Canada as immigrants or refugees. People who live in Canada but who have heritage in other countries may find that the values or ideas they hold from their original culture conflict with those considered to be part of Canadian culture.

Loyalty to Canada and expressing Canadian nationalism can also be difficult because people sometimes struggle to define what it is to be Canadian. People who live in different regions of Canada may feel conflicting loyalties when decisions, issues, celebrations, etc., about Canada conflict with those in their region. For example, people who live in Western Canada sometimes find their loyalties between province and country in conflict. Furthermore, Canada's multicultural makeup can lead to conflicting understandings between different groups because of ethnic nationalism.

Making decisions about which loyalties take precedence can be difficult. Many youths whose families have strong ties to other countries or cultures sometimes struggle to balance these loyalties. For example, young Muslim women living in Canada may feel pressure from their families to wear a hijab in public, even though they are not sure if they would like to maintain this tradition in this country. Reconciling civic nationalism can also be difficult, as people's political beliefs may conflict with the government's decisions about issues at home and abroad. Deciding if and how to support the various political parties in Canada can also be difficult.

Within Canada, members of the Aboriginal populations sometimes struggle to reconcile their loyalties to their own nation and to Canada. At one time in Canada's history, the government tried to assimilate First Nations, Métis, and Inuit people into the predominant white cultures. Although official government policies have abandoned this idea, these groups believe that in order to preserve their culture, they must maintain a feeling of nationhood among their members within the borders of Canada. As a result, some members of these communities feel conflicting loyalties when issues such as land claims and treaty settlements are being discussed.

Another group within Canada that often experiences conflicting nationalistic loyalties is the Québécois population. French Canada's fight for the preservation of their culture and language has long been a part of Canadian history. Some Quebecers believe that Quebec's separation from Canada is the only way to preserve their unique culture. Quebecers often think of themselves as a nation within Canada, and their loyalties to the province often conflict with loyalties to Canada. In addition, there are conflicting loyalties within the province of Quebec. Not all Quebecers and many Anglophones and recent immigrants to Canada who live in Quebec do not support the idea of an independent Quebec and feel more loyalty to Canada than to the province.

Practice Questions: 10 and 11

1.11 evaluate the importance of reconciling nationalism with contending non-nationalist loyalties (religion, region, culture, race, ideology, class, other contending loyalties)

Nationalism and Non-Nationalistic Loyalties

It is important that people are able to reconcile their feelings of nationalism with contending non-nationalistic loyalties. For example, people's religion can be an extremely powerful force in how they make decisions and the actions they take in society. Sometimes, it can be difficult for people to balance their devotion to their religion and devotion to their country. Further, conflicts between people who have different religions but live in the same country can arise. Over humankind's history, many violent events and wars have taken place in the name of religion.

The region in which someone lives can also be a contending loyalty. Sometimes, what is considered best for the country as a whole may have negative consequences for a specific region. In addition, the promotion of the culture or economic prosperity of a region can sometimes clash with the goals of the country.

People's feelings of loyalty to their race or culture may conflict with the loyalties they feel toward the country. Decisions made in a country may conflict with the values or traditions held by people of a specific race or culture.

People's loyalties toward their own ideologies may also conflict with their feelings of nationalism. For example, if the ideologies on which actions taken or policies developed by a country's government are based on conflict with people's personal ideologies, they may have trouble reconciling these conflicting loyalties. It may feel as though supporting the government and the country forces them to sacrifice their own beliefs.

People's class loyalties may conflict with their feelings of nationalism. They may not have a sense of belonging if they feel they are not a part of a country because of feelings of separation caused by their social status. In addition, demands for change to social status or for greater economic opportunity can cause conflict and sometimes violence.

Practice Questions: 12 and 13

PRACTICE QUESTIONS—RELATED ISSUE 1

1. The **most important** ingredient in Canadian nationalism is a shared

A. culture

B. identity

C. territory

D. language

Use the following information to answer the next question.

> Civic nationalism binds people together through a shared belief in the same laws, values, and political traditions. It is capable of uniting people who do not share the same race, ethnicity, culture, or language.

2. Based on the given definition, in which of the following situations would civic nationalism **most likely** be expressed?

A. During the campaign period leading up to a national election

B. During a referendum about the potential for Quebec sovereignty within Canada

C. After the gold medal win of the Canadian women's hockey team at the Olympics

D. During negotiations between First Nations peoples and the Canadian government over treaty rights

3. Which of the following types of nationalism is **most useful** for promoting national unity in a bilingual, multi-racial, and multicultural country such as Canada?

A. Civic nationalism

B. Tribal nationalism

C. Ethnic nationalism

D. Cultural nationalism

Use the following information to answer the next question.

Our people have lived on this land for centuries. It is part of what defines us as a people. Our survival, culture, and traditions are based around our use and worship of the land. It is the most important part of our heritage.

4. Which of the following groups of Canadians has **most likely** developed the sense of nationalism from their relationship to the land described in this statement?

A. Inuit

B. Québécois

C. Western Canadians

D. Recent immigrants to Canada

5. Which of the following types of nationalism would be **most successful** in maintaining the unity of a culturally diverse nation-state?

A. Linguistic

B. Religious

C. Ethnic

D. Civic

6. Which of the following types of nationalism is **least likely** to be present in a nation?

A. Ethnic

B. Cultural

C. Patriotic

D. Spiritual

7. Which event from the French Revolution is generally considered to be the **first** public demonstration of the power of modern nationalism?

A. The March on Versailles

B. The execution of Louis XVI

C. The Storming of the Bastille

D. The summoning of the Estates-General

8. Which of the following statements accurately describes the social conditions in France prior to the French Revolution?

   A. Wealth was equally distributed, and French citizens were satisfied with the status quo.

   B. There was a rigid class structure and significant inequities in wealth between these classes.

   C. French citizens did not experience great wealth, but the government provided them with necessities.

   D. The government of France was heavily in debt, largely because of its support of the American Revolution.

9. French-speaking Quebecers stopped identifying themselves as "French Canadians" shortly after the onset of

   A. the October Crisis

   B. the Quiet Revolution

   C. the Northwest Rebellion of 1885

   D. conscription during the First World War

Use the following information to answer the next question.

The Minister of Intergovernmental Affairs has recommended that Quebec be guaranteed a minimum of 25 per cent of the seats in the House of Commons in perpetuity, in order to ensure the survival of Quebec's French language and unique culture.

10. Which of the following groups would **most likely** oppose the given recommendation?

   A. Members of Parliament from Quebec

   B. Canadian voters who live inside Quebec

   C. Members of Quebec's national assembly

   D. Canadian voters who live outside Quebec

11. In which of the following situations is it likely that French Canadians were **most conflicted** between loyalty to Quebec and loyalty to Canada?

   A. Gold medal wins for both of Canada's hockey teams at the 2002 Olympics

   B. The introduction of the Official Languages Act

   C. Canada's involvement in the Korean War

   D. The Conscription Crisis of 1917

Use the following information to answer the next two questions.

Speaker I
I have lived in Canada all my life and I still have trouble deciding how loyal I am to the country. Sometimes, the policies adopted by the Canadian government are in such opposition to my personal political beliefs that I feel like I am hardly part of the country I live in.

Speaker II
I am a Canadian but I am also a citizen of Israel. Being Jewish is such an important part of who I am, and sometimes I don't feel like I connect with other Canadians. I feel like I have more of a connection to people living halfway around the world. I love Canada, but my faith is really the most important thing in my life.

Speaker III
I am a Québécois before I am a Canadian. Living in Quebec and living the lifestyle of a French-Canadian is very important to me. Even though I am proud to be a Canadian, I feel more connected to Quebec than to Canada as a whole.

Speaker IV
My people have lived in Canada before it was even known as such. Our history is such a major part of the development of Canada and yet it seems like other people don't care to know it. I am proud to be a First Nations person, but sometimes I feel like that doesn't necessarily mean I am Canadian.

12. Which of the given speakers describes religion as a contending loyalty to his or her feelings of nationalism?

A. Speaker I

B. Speaker II

C. Speaker III

D. Speaker IV

13. Consideration of which of the following areas causes Speaker III to feel divided about his or her loyalty to Canada?

A. Race

B. Class

C. Region

D. Religion

ANSWERS AND SOLUTIONS—PRACTICE QUESTIONS

1. B	4. A	7. C	10. D	13. C
2. A	5. D	8. B	11. D	
3. A	6. C	9. B	12. B	

1. B

A shared group identity is the basis of nationalism and nationhood. Nationalism exists whenever a group views itself as a nation. Nationalism can exist when a group shares a common identity but does not share a common culture, territory, or language.

A shared culture, territory, or language is less important in maintaining nationalism than is a shared group identity. There are many examples of nations that have lost their culture, territory, or language but continued to share a national identity—for example, the Jewish, Irish, and Palestinian nations have all experienced this.

2. A

Civic nationalism would most likely be expressed during a time when Canadians of various cultures and ethnicities share a common civic goal, such as choosing a leader for the national government.

Situations such as successes in international sports do not usually spur feelings of nationalism related to government and politics. Discussions of treaty rights (between First Nations peoples and governments) and Quebec sovereignty would likely spur feelings of ethnic or cultural nationalism because the groups of people involved share a common culture, language, and traditions.

3. A

Civic nationalism binds people together through a shared belief in the same laws, values, and political traditions. It is capable of uniting people who do not share the same race, ethnicity, culture, or language.

The terms *tribal nationalism* and *cultural nationalism* are synonymous with the term *ethnic nationalism*. These types of nationalism unite individuals who share the same ancestry or cultural traditions. Consequently, they would not be effective instruments for unifying Canada's linguistically and culturally diverse population.

4. A

The Inuit culture is strongly tied to the land in Northern Canada. Generations of Inuit people have lived in the same region for centuries, and much of their culture, traditions, and economic survival depends on the land.

Although the Québécois have loyalty to the province of Quebec, the nationhood felt among Québécois people is less associated with the land and their relationship to it than to the French language and cultural traditions. Western Canadians often feel a sense of loyalty to the land, as many Westerners have an agricultural history. However, the sense of nationhood described in the source is generally not felt by Western Canadians. Recent immigrants to Canada do not have a history with the land, and therefore their sense of Canadian nationalism does not stem from their relationship to the land.

5. D

A nation-state is a sovereign country, which means it has its own government and political systems. Civic nationalism is based on a common dedication to particular types of political traditions, laws, and values. In a culturally diverse nation-state, civic nationalism is able to provide a sense of unity among people of different cultures, languages, and ethnicities.

Linguistic, religious, or ethnic nationalism would not serve as well to unite people in a culturally diverse nation-state.

6. C

Patriotic nationalism is based on a common love for one's country, and because a nation is not a sovereign country, this type of nationalism would not likely be present.

As *nation* can refer to groups of people with similar cultures, traditions, and languages who inhabit a specific area but do not have the ability to govern themselves, each of ethnic, spiritual, and cultural nationalism would likely be present.

7. C

Nationalism is a force that harnesses "people power" by convincing individuals they are part of a larger group (i.e., the nation) in which people share a common national identity and common national goals. With the Storming of the Bastille, French nationalists demonstrated that nothing could thwart the power of the people once the nation had been aroused and united behind a common cause. The novelty of Bastille Day had a great impact on the imagination of Europeans at the time and is generally considered to be the birthday of modern nationalism.

The March on Versailles was an example of modern nationalism, but it occurred after the Storming of the Bastille. Neither the execution of Louis XVI nor the summoning of the Estates-General was an example of modern nationalism.

8. B

In pre-revolutionary France, there were strict distinctions between the First, Second, and Third Estates. These distinctions led to the serious inequities in wealth and status that contributed to the unrest leading up to the French Revolution. Citizens began to band together to demand change, fostering feelings of nationalism.

Wealth was not equally distributed in France, as members of the Third Estate were often extremely poor. There were even differences in wealth between the First and Second Estates. The government of France did not provide the necessities for its citizens, as many French people were starving and living in atrocious conditions. Although the French government was largely in debt, this was not a social condition, rather an economic one.

9. B

Between 1867 and 1960, Quebecers referred to themselves as French Canadians. During the Quiet Revolution of the 1960s, they began to call themselves "Québécois" instead. This change was one sign of rising Québécois nationalism in Quebec and a signal that Canadian nationalism was in retreat in the province.

Thus change was not a result of any one of these three events. For example, Quebecers were referring to themselves as *Québécois* before the October Crisis erupted in 1970.

10. D

Of the groups listed, Canadian voters who live outside Quebec would be most likely to oppose the recommendation because it could potentially decrease their voting power in the future.

Members of Parliament from Quebec, members of Quebec's national assembly, and Canadian voters who live inside Quebec would be more likely to support the proposal because it could potentially maintain Quebec's influential position in Canadian politics despite Quebec's low rate of population growth relative to the rest of the country.

11. D

During the Conscription Crisis of 1917, French Canadians experienced great conflict between their loyalty to Quebec and their loyalty to Canada. Many French Canadians resented being forced to fight in a war they believed to be Britain's fight, not Canada's, and certainly not Quebec's.

It is very unlikely that the gold medal wins for Canada at the 2002 Winter Olympics, the introduction of the Official Languages Act in 1988, and Canada's involvement in the Korean War would have caused as much conflict of loyalties as the Conscription Crisis of 1917.

12. B

Speaker II is Jewish and explains that being loyal to his or her religion sometimes conflicts with his or her loyalties to Canada.

Speaker I describes ideology as a competing loyalty. Speaker III describes region as a competing loyalty. Speaker IV describes race as a competing loyalty.

13. C

Speaker III describes loyalty to Quebec (a region in Canada) as contending with a feeling of loyalty to Canada.

Being Québécois does not define a person's race, religion, or class.

UNIT TEST— RELATED ISSUE 1

1. When Canadian athletes win Olympic medals, Canada's identity is strengthened because it
   A. increases national pride
   B. encourages young people to be more physically active
   C. gains more international recognition for Canada's athletes
   D. demonstrates that Canadians are very much like people from other countries

Use the following information to answer the next question.

> "Canada proved herself on the Western Front at Vimy Ridge, Passchendaele and Amiens. For the first time in Canada's history, Canadians had accomplished world-class feats of greatness. They had achieved something that made Canadians proud of being Canadian and made other nationalities sit up and take notice. After these three triumphs, Canada was no longer regarded merely as the junior-partner of Great Britain. It had crossed the point of no return on its journey toward complete self-determination."

2. Which of the following ingredients of nationhood is **not** referred to in the given passage?
   A. Patriotic pride
   B. National consciousness
   C. International recognition
   D. Effective control of national borders

3. The term *national identity* is **most closely** related to the term
   A. nationality
   B. nationalism
   C. national culture
   D. national consciousness.

Use the following information to answer the next question.

Speaker I	The glue that holds a nation together is ethnicity. National unity is based on blood ties.
Speaker II	Every nationality must have the right of self-determination. Ultimately this means it should have its own nation-state.
Speaker III	People should put their loyalty to the nation ahead of all other loyalties. In particular, loyalty to the national community should supersede loyalties to family, locality, region, or class.
Speaker IV	The best foundation for a nation is shared values. People constitute a nation whenever they agree to respect the same laws, protect the equal rights of fellow citizens, and fulfil common duties of citizenship.

4. Which speaker expresses ideas associated **exclusively** with civic nationalism?
   A. Speaker I
   B. Speaker II
   C. Speaker III
   D. Speaker IV

Use the following information to answer the next two questions.

Speaker I	Nationalism has been a major cause of military conflicts during the past two hundred years. Before the rise of nationalism, wars were fought on a much smaller scale. Nationalism also gave rise to the concept of "total war" in which all members of an opposing nation—both soldiers and civilians—are considered to be enemies. Nationalism is like racism: it is a negative force that should always be resisted and discouraged.
Speaker II	Nationalism is acceptable up to a point. It can benefit people by making them more neighbourly. It helps individuals to see strangers as national brothers and sisters who are worthy of respect. This perception greatly reduces internal strife within a nation. Nationalism crosses the line when it causes a people to regard foreigners with contempt. Ethnic nationalists are more prone to negative nationalism than are civic nationalists, but even civic nationalists go astray on occasion.
Speaker III	Two of the greatest villains of modern history—Maximilien Robespierre and Adolf Hitler—were fanatical nationalists. Their infamous atrocities—the Reign of Terror and the Holocaust—both resulted from excessive nationalism. The biographers of Robespierre and Hitler have demonstrated that both types of nationalism (civic and ethnic) have the potential to turn into ultranationalism, which is the dark side of nationalism. Nationalism should never be taken to the extreme. The nation should never be elevated above God, morality, ethics, or human rights. Nationalism is a man-made ideology, and as such, is imperfect. The cult of nationalism, like other cults, can give rise to grave social and political disorders.
Speaker IV	One of the most-admired social forces is team spirit. In organized sports young people are encouraged to work together for the good of the team. In the armed forces, soldiers are trained to look out for one another on the battlefield. In corporations, all employees are motivated to work for the greater good of the company. Nationalism is nothing more (and nothing less) than the encouragement of team spirit among a much larger group of people. This is why the state must promote nationalism as much as possible. Without nationalism, citizens would have no incentive to work for the general progress of their nation. Without nationalism, people would not feel at home within their own country.

5. Which of the following issues is being addressed by all of the given speakers?
   A. Does nationalism cause wars?
   B. To what extent should nationalism be encouraged?
   C. Should all nations have the right of self-determination?
   D. Should governments promote civic nationalism or ethnic nationalism?

6. The type of nationalism being promoted by Speaker IV is
   - **A.** linguistic nationalism
   - **B.** religious nationalism
   - **C.** patriotic nationalism
   - **D.** spiritual nationalism

Use the following information to answer the next question.

It is said that in order to be a good patriot, one has to be the enemy of the rest of mankind. To be a good patriot is to wish that one's country might be enriched by trade, and be powerful by arms. It is clear that one country cannot gain without another's losing, and that one cannot conquer without bringing misery to another. Such then is the human state at the present time, that to wish greatness for one's country is to wish harm to one's neighbours. It would be much better if a person wished that his fatherland might never be greater, smaller, richer, or poorer than any other country. This wish would make a person something better than a patriot; it would make him a citizen of the world.

Voltaire

7. The given quotation is **primarily** an attack on
   - **A.** ultranationalism
   - **B.** civic nationalism
   - **C.** ethnic nationalism
   - **D.** cultural nationalism

Use the following information to answer the next two questions.

8. The given cartoon depicts the rapid growth of German and Russian nationalism during the period from 1805 to1813. What leader was responsible for this growth?
   - **A.** Catherine the Great
   - **B.** Frederick the Great
   - **C.** Napoleon Bonaparte
   - **D.** The first Duke of Wellington

9. The given cartoon depicts the growth of
   A. civic nationalism in Europe
   B. ethnic nationalism in Europe
   C. liberal nationalism in Europe
   D. revolutionary democratic nationalism in Europe

Use the following information to answer the next question.

Goal I
Suppress radicalism

Goal II
Combat civic nationalism

Goal III
Stop the spread of liberal ideas

Goal IV
Prevent the weakening of empires by ethnic nationalism

10. Actions to prevent the growth of feelings of nationhood among French citizens whose priorities were to achieve a democratic French republic would be encompassed by which of the given goals?
   A. Goal I
   B. Goal II
   C. Goal III
   D. Goal IV

11. For a Québécois nationalist, which of the following potential loyalties **most likely** conflicts with his or her feelings of Canadian nationalism?
   A. Ideology
   B. Region
   C. Class
   D. Race

12. Which of the following people would be **most likely** to feel a conflict between loyalties to his or her race and to Canada?
   A. A Muslim Canadian
   B. A Québécois Canadian
   C. A Communist Canadian
   D. A First Nations Canadian

Use the following information to answer the next three questions.

Group I	Our common belief in God and his laws is what makes us feel united. Even though we don't all live in the same country or speak the same language, we feel a sense of connectedness with each other because of our faith.
Group II	We are so proud of the democracy that exists in our country. It is so important for people to have a say in what happens in government and for that government to be accountable to the people. Our laws and political traditions are what make our country great.
Group III	There is no greater country on Earth than Canada! From our beautiful environment to our rich cultural differences to our international reputation, Canada is envied around the world. Even though we are all different, we would do almost anything to protect our country.
Group IV	Even though some governments may not recognize us as a nation, we are a nation! We share a common culture and loyalty to our land, and one day we will govern ourselves and be free of the people who currently control us.

13. Members of which of the given groups share feelings of political nationalism?

A. Group I

B. Group II

C. Group III

D. Group IV

14. Members of which of the given groups share feelings of patriotic nationalism?

A. Group I

B. Group II

C. Group III

D. Group IV

15. Jewish people around the world would **most likely** share the type of nationalism described by group

A. I

B. II

C. III

D. IV

16. Which of the following factors would have the **most** influence on the disparity that can exist in a collective consciousness about nationalism in a society?

A. Shared history

B. Immigration trends

C. Linguistic similarities

D. Religious homogeneity

Use the following information to answer the next three questions.

Speaker I
We live in Fort McMurray and have lived here since long before the oil boom. The oil industry is such a big part of our lives and really helps define who we are. However, the more I hear about the damage being done to the environment and how big a part the oil industry plays in that damage, the more I start to wonder what is best for our province and country in the long run.

Speaker II
I love living in Canada. I moved here from the Saudi Arabia two years ago and am happy to live in a place where everyone's differences are appreciated and sometimes not even noticed! However, I struggle sometimes to define myself, as I don't want to let go of my heritage. Some of my traditions and beliefs are vastly different from the "norm" here.

Speaker III
It's time the poor people of Alberta stand up for themselves. All I hear about in the news is the "Alberta Advantage" and the "hot economy." I've been out of work for months and can hardly pay my rent. The government seems uninterested into hearing what I have to say, and sometimes I wonder if I'm valued as an Albertan. I think it's time we worked together to demand real change for the underprivileged in our province.

Speaker IV
Being a Quebecer is part of my identity and my beliefs about who I am. I am proud of the French culture in Canada and the role we have played in shaping this country. However, I don't know if separation from Canada is the answer—how can we say we are one of the founding peoples and then abandon the very place we helped to found?

17. The speaker who describes feeling conflicting loyalty between ethnic nationalism and Canadian nationalism is

A. Speaker I

B. Speaker II

C. Speaker III

D. Speaker IV

18. The speaker whose views **most closely** echo those that fuelled the French Revolution is

A. Speaker I

B. Speaker II

C. Speaker III

D. Speaker IV

19. Which of the following statements about Speaker IV is most likely **true**?

A. The speaker is not supportive of federalism in Canada.

B. The speaker voted "no" in the 1995 Quebec referendum.

C. The speaker would have supported the ideals of the FLQ.

D. The speaker agrees with the platform of the Bloc Québécois.

ANSWERS AND SOLUTIONS—UNIT TEST

1. A	**5. B**	**9. B**	**13. D**	**17. B**
2. D	**6. C**	**10. B**	**14. C**	**18. C**
3. D	**7. A**	**11. B**	**15. A**	**19. B**
4. D	**8. C**	**12. D**	**16. B**	

1. A

Sporting achievements generally boost national pride in Canada and other countries. National pride (nationalism) tends to make people more aware of their identity as members of a nation.

Physical fitness and international recognition are not as important for the development of a Canadian national consciousness. Furthermore, demonstrating that Canadians are much like people of other nationalities would tend to erode national identity—it would certainly not enhance Canadian national consciousness.

2. D

The quotation does not mention Canada's effective control of national borders.

The passage refers to patriotic pride ("They had achieved something that made Canadians proud of being Canadian"), national consciousness ("It had crossed the point of no return on its journey toward complete self-determination"), and international recognition ("After these three triumphs, Canada was no longer regarded merely as the junior-partner of Great Britain.").

3. D

The term *national consciousness* refers to a people's awareness of their nationhood. When a nation has achieved a national consciousness, it has developed a national identity.

The terms *nationality*, *nationalism*, and *national culture* are closely related to the term *national identity*, but not as closely as the term *national consciousness*.

4. D

Civic nationalism is based on political and legal equality between citizens, respect for laws, and shared values. Speaker IV refers to these founding principles of civic nationalism.

Speaker I expresses the views of an ethnic nationalist (cultural nationalist). Speakers II and III express basic nationalist views that would be accepted by either ethnic nationalists or civic nationalists.

5. B

All four speakers address the question "To what extent should nationalism be encouraged?" Speaker I argues that nationalism should always be discouraged. Speaker II maintains that nationalism should be encouraged to a certain degree, provided it does not lead to xenophobia (fear and hatred of foreigners). Speaker III suggests that extreme nationalism should never be encouraged. Speaker IV states that nationalism should be encouraged as much as possible.

None of the questions "Does nationalism cause wars?" "Should all nations have the right of self-determination?" and "Should governments promote civic nationalism or ethnic nationalism?" are being addressed.

6. C

The speaker suggests that patriotic nationalism (love for one's country) is important in order for a nation's citizens to have feelings of nationhood and a willingness to advance the country.

Religious, linguistic, and spiritual nationalisms are not being promoted by Speaker IV.

7. A

Voltaire's statement criticizes ultranationalism (extreme nationalism). Voltaire does not believe that people should go to any length to gain power or glory for their nation. He believes in a style of nationalism that respects the rights of other nations. Ultranationalists have no respect for the rights of other nations; in fact, they tend to regard all foreigners as enemies of their nation.

Voltaire does not directly condemn ethnic nationalism, cultural nationalism, or civic nationalism in the quotation.

8. C

Napoleon Bonaparte provoked the rise of modern German and Russian nationalism through his many attacks, wars, and invasions on these two countries. National consciousness emerged among the citizens of Germany and Russia as a reaction to defeats and humiliations inflicted by Napoleon's troops and officials.

Neither Catherine the Great, Frederick the Great, nor the first Duke of Wellington caused the growth of nationalism in Germany and Russia.

9. B

In the cartoon, only Russian and German nationalism grows. The type of nationalism embraced by the Russians and Germans was ethnic nationalism. Ethnic nationalism was based on the sharing of common cultural, linguistic, and ancestral bonds. It was a reaction to and a rejection of the French-style civic nationalism that was founded upon shared liberal values and a belief in political and legal equality.

The cartoon does not depict the growth of civic, liberal, or revolutionary democratic nationalism in Europe. *Revolutionary democratic nationalism* and *liberal nationalism* mean the same thing as *civic nationalism*.

10. B

Civic nationalism binds people together through a shared belief in the same laws, values, and political traditions, which would be the goals of people who shared a desire for a democratic French republic.

People whose main priority was a democratic French republic would be unlikely to take actions to suppress radicalism, stop the spread of liberal ideas, or suppress ethnic nationalism.

11. B

Québécois nationalism is based on various loyalties including feelings of loyalty to a region—the province of Quebec.

Generally, Québécois nationalism is not based on feelings of loyalty to ideology, race, or class.

12. D

People's loyalty to their race can conflict with loyalties to their country, and this can occur for First Nations Canadians, who may struggle to define themselves more as Canadian or more as First Nations.

Muslims, Québécois, and Communists are not races but religious, cultural, and ideological groups, respectively.

13. D

Political nationalism is when people share a desire to govern themselves independently without outside influence. Group IV describes a desire for such autonomy, and this desire is what creates a sense of nationhood among them.

Group I describes religious nationalism. Group II describes civic nationalism. Group III describes patriotic nationalism.

14. C

Patriotic nationalism is when people share a love for their country, regardless of their cultural, racial, or linguistic differences. Group III suggests the people who share feelings of love for Canada are all different and yet feel a sense of nationhood with each other.

Group I describes religious nationalism. Group II describes civic nationalism. Group IV describes political nationalism.

15. A

Group I describes religious nationalism, which is a sense of nationhood among people who share the same religion even if they do not live in the same country. Often, Jewish people around the world have a sense of nationhood with each other even if their daily lives are vastly different—their common religious beliefs spur feelings of nationalism among them.

Group II describes civic nationalism, Group III describes patriotic nationalism, and Group IV describes political nationalism, none of which have religion as a defining factor.

16. B

Immigration trends can contribute to disparity in a collective consciousness, as people from different backgrounds may have different loyalties or levels of patriotism in a country.

Shared history, linguistic similarities, and religious homogeneity tend to unite people's collective consciousness rather than cause disparity.

17. B

Speaker II describes feeling conflicted between being loyal to his or her ethnic heritage in Saudi Arabia and embracing the traditions and cultures of Canada.

Speaker I describes conflicts between nationalism and ideological beliefs. Speaker III describes conflicts between nationalism and class. Speaker IV describes conflict between Québécois nationalism and Canadian nationalism.

18. C

Speaker III describes conflicts between nationalism and class by describing the frustrations felt by those who are not part of the middle or upper classes. Anger over similar issues in France prior to the Revolution helped fuel the feelings that led to demands for change in the social and economic structure of French society.

Speaker I describes conflict between ideology and nationalism. Speaker II describes conflict between ethnicity and nationalism. Speaker IV describes conflict between Québécois nationalism and Canadian nationalism. None of speakers I, II, or IV describe situations similar to that in France prior to the Revolution.

19. B

Although Speaker IV clearly states that he or she has feelings of Québécois nationalism, the speaker does not believe that separatism for Quebec is appropriate and therefore would have voted "no" in the referendum, which posed the question as to whether Quebec should seek independence from Canada.

Because the speaker is not supportive of separatism, he or she would likely not have supported the FLQ, would likely support federalism, and likely does not agree with the platform of the Bloc Québécois, which is a separatist party.

Related Issue 2

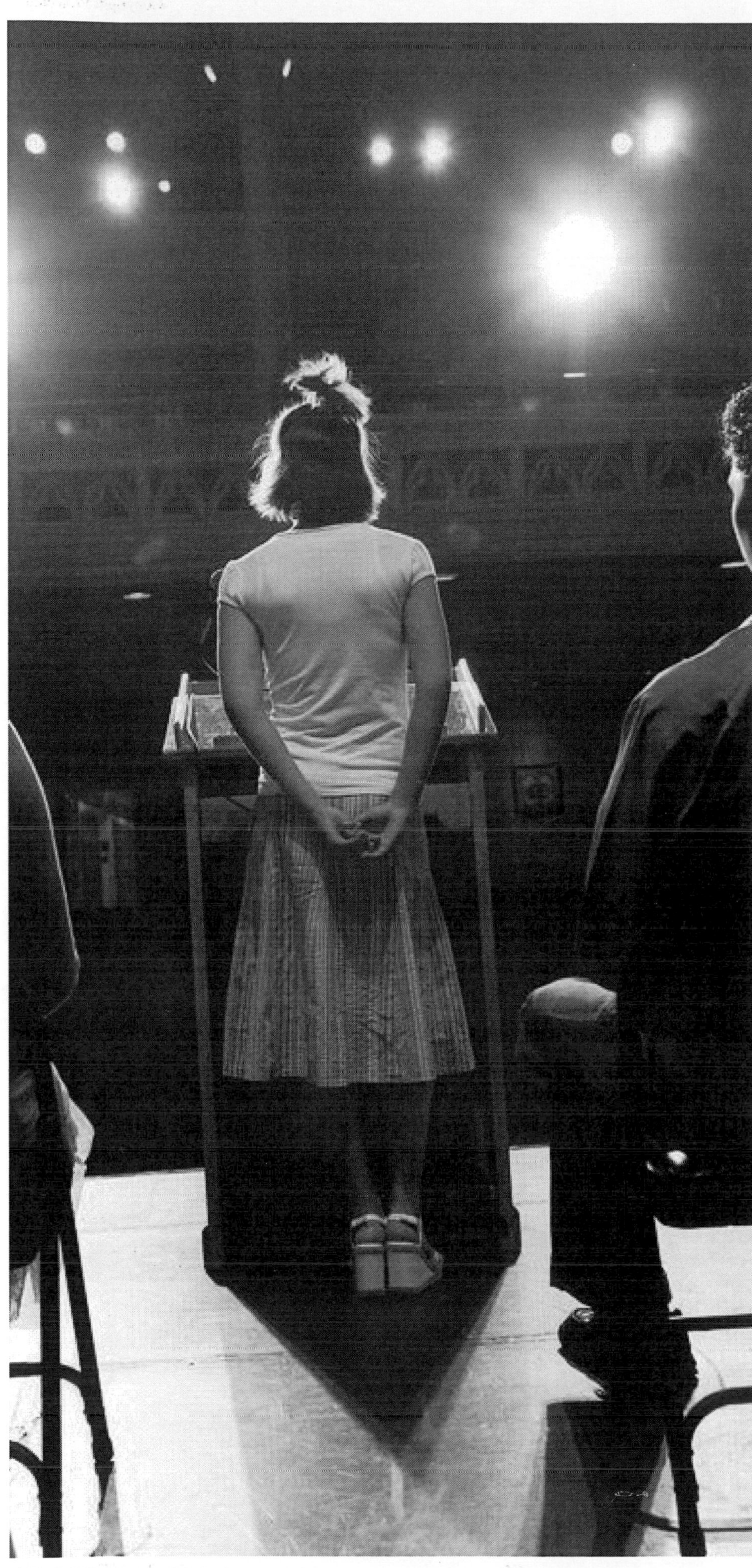

RELATED ISSUE 2

Table of Correlations

Specific Outcome	Practice Questions	Unit Test Questions	Practice Test 1	Practice Test 2
Students will assess impacts of nationalism, ultranationalism and the pursuit of national interest.				
2.4 explore the relationship between nationalism and the pursuit of national interest	1, 2	20	7	24
2.5 analyze how the pursuit of national interest shapes foreign policy (First World War peace settlements, the interwar period)	3, 4	1, 2, 7, 9	5, 18, 20, 33	7, 8, 19, 20, 21
2.6 analyze the relationship between nationalism and ultranationalism	5, 6	3, 19	3	
2.7 analyze nationalism and ultranationalism during times of conflict (causes of the First and Second World Wars, examples of nationalism and ultranationalism from the First and Second World Wars, ultranationalism in Japan, internments in Canada, conscription crises)	7, 8	4, 8, 15,16, 17,18	17, 19, 21, 22, 32	16, 17, 22, 23, 25
2.8 analyze ultranationalism as a cause of genocide (the Holocaust, 1932–1933 famine in Ukraine, contemporary examples)	9, 10	6, 10, 11	34, 35, 38, 39	36, 37, 38, 39
2.9 analyze impacts of the pursuit of national self-determination (successor states; decolonization; Québécois nationalism and sovereignty movement; First Nations, Métis and Inuit self-government; contemporary examples)	11, 12	5, 12, 13, 14	36, 37	40, 41

RELATED ISSUE 2

To What Extent Should National Interest be Pursued?

2.4 explore the relationship between nationalism and the pursuit of national interest

Nationalism and the Pursuit of National Interest

The phrase **pursuit of national interest** refers to the efforts made by a country to ensure that actions taken both domestically and internationally benefit the country as a whole. **Nationalism**, the feeling of pride in one's country, can have an effect on how leaders and citizens pursue the nation's interests as they try to ensure the best possible situation for the nation. Countries make both domestic and international policies to help achieve the goals of the country; that is, to pursue the country's national interests. Often, feelings of entitlement or the belief that a country deserves respect or certain treatments drive this pursuit. Sometimes, a nation's pursuit of its own interests can come at the expense of the well-being of other nations or even of citizens within the country.

Practice Questions: 1 and 2

2.5 analyze how the pursuit of national interest shapes foreign policy (First World War peace settlements, the interwar period)

The Pursuit of National Interest and Foreign Policy

Foreign policy, which is comprised of the decisions made by a government that dictate its behaviours on an international scale, is largely shaped by a nation's pursuit of national interest. Each government holds certain goals for its country, and, therefore, its interactions with other nations are dictated by a desire to achieve these goals. Following the First World War, each of the Big Three leaders (David Lloyd George of Great Britain, Woodrow Wilson of the United States, and Georges Clemenceau of France) had specific goals they wanted to achieve for their country following the destruction caused by the First World War, and the actions each man took at the 1919 Paris Peace Conference at Versailles were attempts to achieve these goals. For example, after being decimated by Germany during the war, France wanted to ensure this would never happen again. To this end, France lobbied heavily for harsh monetary punishment of Germany and strict regulation of the German military so that Germany would be in such a position that it would never be able to attack France again. At the Versailles peace talks, some countries attempted to enhance their own national security by creating and joining a collective international organization: the League of Nations. The decision to be part of an international organization demonstrated a shift in these nations' foreign policy toward internationalism.

In spite of that, for some nations, the interwar period was characterized by the pursuit of national interest as the driving force behind foreign policies. Although the United States was not physically damaged by the First World War, the loss of American soldiers during the war led to an attitude that the United States should be more concerned with domestic affairs and stay out of the affairs of other countries. As a result, the United States adopted a policy of isolationism. The United States rejected various postwar treaties, did not join the newly formed League of Nations, and raised tariffs on European imports. Although isolationism is considered to have been the foreign policy of the United States during the interwar period, it is important to note that during this time, the United States did take some actions that contradicted this policy. Some of these actions included the development of the Dawes and Young plans and participation in the Kellogg–Briand Pact. France continued to pursue its policy of national security by seeking military alliances with other countries and by initiating agreements such as the Kellogg–Briand Pact. In addition, France constructed the Maginot Line, a series of fortifications along its borders with Germany and Italy. Great Britain's foreign policy centred on avoiding war, which resulted in the adoption of a policy of appeasement when faced with aggressive actions from other countries. For example, Great Britain chose not to challenge Hitler when Germany marched troops into the Rhineland and when it took over Austria, both of which went directly against international treaties ratified by Great Britain. Historians view Britain's policy of appeasement and subsequent lack of action as one of the main causes of the Second World War.

Following the First World War, some countries took actions to further their national interests through aggressive foreign policies. Examples include Italy's desire to be recognized as an international power, which led to the development of Fascism within the country and imperialistic policies and actions, such as the invasion of Abyssinia in 1935. The Soviet Union also wanted to achieve international recognition and improve its national security, as it too had been ravaged by the First World War. As a result, when Stalin came to power, he initiated policies aimed at making the Soviet Union an economic powerhouse through the development of communist policies aimed at centralizing almost all aspects of the economy. In addition, Stalin spent a lot of money on the military and, although he was eventually betrayed, developed an alliance with Hitler. Japan's foreign policy of imperialism stemmed from a need for resources and an inability to secure them through legitimate means. Japan took aggressive action against many of its Asian neighbours and caused international tension when it refused to back down in the face of the League of Nations' requests after Japan invaded Manchuria in 1931.

Germany was economically and morally crushed after the signing of the Treaty of Versailles in 1919. The democratic government of the Weimar Republic sought alliance with Russia through the Treaty of Rapallo, which caused tension with France. The people of Germany were desperate and felt betrayed by their government, which led to the climate of support for Hitler's Nazi party and its extreme views. Germany's foreign policy soon became one of restoring Germany's greatness through militaristic and imperialistic actions, which led to serious international tension and, eventually, the Second World War.

Practice Questions: 3 and 4

2.6 analyze the relationship between nationalism and ultranationalism

NATIONALISM AND ULTRANATIONALISM

As has already been established, **nationalism** can be defined as a feeling of pride, devotion, and loyalty to one's country or nation/nation-state, but when it is taken to the extreme, **ultranationalism** can develop. This form of nationalism exists when feelings of pride and devotion result in actions or policies that are detrimental to the citizens of that country or to other nations. Governments with ultranationalistic policies may punish or execute people who they deem unsupportive of their policies or those who they feel do not put the well-being of the state before themselves. The foreign policies of such countries may include the desire to take over nations that are located on lands the ultranationalistic government believes are rightly theirs or nations that have resources that would benefit the ultranationalistic country. Where nationalism exists, people are free to express their devotion to their country, but where ultranationalism exists, people are expected to do so even if they do not feel that way. Ultranationalistic states often develop in countries where there are extreme economic hardships and citizens are looking for a leader with solutions, even if those solutions are not something the populace would support under normal circumstances. Ultranationalistic countries are usually led by one person or a ruling elite that has almost complete control over the decision-making processes in a country. Militaristic and racist policies and the use of propaganda in these states are common, as is the development of fascist governments, such as those in Nazi Germany and Fascist Italy.

Practice Questions: 5 and 6

2.7 analyze nationalism and ultranationalism during times of conflict (causes of the First and Second World Wars, examples of nationalism and ultranationalism from the First and Second World Wars, ultranationalism in Japan, internments in Canada, conscription crises)

Nationalism and Ultranationalism During Times of Conflict

During times of conflict, people can more easily cross the boundaries between nationalism and ultranationalism than during times of peace and prosperity. This is because a real or perceived threat usually results in fear and the desire to protect one's country and traditions. Nationalism and ultranationalism have been at the root of many major conflicts throughout history, including most notably, the First and Second World wars.

Prior to the First World War, Europe had undergone a major shift in beliefs about how government should be organized and how much power citizens should have in the decision-making process. As a result of the French Revolution and Napoleonic Era, feelings of nationalism began to develop and minorities under the control of large empires began to resent the control held over them. Movements for independence became prevalent. Despite efforts to quell these movements, monarchs and leaders of empires were unable to stop the wave of nationalistic feelings sweeping across Europe. Tensions among different nationalities within empires weakened leaders' control and led to small outbreaks of violence, such as those in the Balkan region. Known as the "powder keg of Europe," the Balkan region had experienced several wars when different groups attempted to assert independence in the face of imperialism by larger countries. It was in this region that the event that sparked the First World War occurred: a young Serbian nationalist assassinated Archduke Ferdinand of Austria and his wife in protest of Austrian attempts to control the Balkan region.

Prior to the outbreak of the First World War, nationalism had also been developing during the late 1800s and early 1900s as empires attempted to improve their international prestige and increase their economic power by instituting policies of imperialism through which they forcibly took over various parts of Africa and Asia. In addition, nationalism grew as empires sought to demonstrate military strength through the build up of armies and weaponry. As well, prior to the First World War, European nations concerned about their own national security forged multiple alliances with other European nations. As a result, within weeks of the initial conflict, dozens of countries were pulled into the First World War as a result of the obligations of these alliances. The nationalistic desire for self-determination also contributed to the war: countries such as the newly formed Italy sought to find ways to claim territory they believed to be rightfully theirs. Nationalism continued to fuel the war and government policies as countries became frantic to preserve their national security.

In Canada, the government used propaganda campaigns to encourage involvement in the war, both on the home front and abroad. Eventually though, in order to get enough recruits, Prime Minister Robert Borden passed the Conscription Act in 1917. This act allowed the government to force people into military service. Conscription caused much tension within Canada because some people did not support the war, believing it to be Britain's fight and not something with which Canada should be involved. First Nations people had no ties to Europe whatsoever, and some believed they should not be forced to fight in this war. Many people on the prairies were angry with conscription because the loss of young men to the war made life on their farms extremely difficult, especially since the government was demanding an increase in the production of wheat and other products needed for the war effort. Ultranationalism began to develop in Canada because the government, fearing that some people living in the country had lineage ties to enemy countries, used internment camps to combat this perceived enemy. From 1914 to 1920, the Canadian government interned citizens who had emigrated from areas under the control of the Austro–Hungarian Empire, primarily those of Ukrainian descent. The internees were placed in forced-labour camps across the country, where they were forced to work on many projects; for example, much of the original infrastructure in Banff National Park was completed with the forced labour of these internees.

The war also resulted in a surge in Canadian nationalistic sentiments. Canadians were proud of military achievements, such as the Canadian Corps success at Vimy Ridge, which garnered international recognition and led other countries to begin to see Canada as a sovereign nation separate from Great Britain. At the peace talks following the First World War, Canada had its own seat, representing itself for the first time in an international arena. These events led to increased feelings of nationalism among Canadians and paved the way for further gains of sovereignty and international recognition in the future.

Ultranationalism played a role in the causes of the Second World War, with the development of fascist governments in Italy and Germany as well as imperialistic policies in Europe and the Far East. After the First World War, Germany had been severely punished by the Treaty of Versailles and within a few years, its humiliated citizens were experiencing severe economic hardships. As a result of hyperinflation in 1923, many German citizens lost everything and began to look for radical solutions to extreme problems. Adolf Hitler gained support from the people by stirring nationalistic feelings, providing a reason for their problems (using the Jews as a scapegoat), and proposing a solution (follow Hitler's policies to achieve greatness for Germany). Propaganda was used to create feelings of ultranationalism in the country, and this in turn resulted in much of the populace accepting policies and actions they likely would not have accepted under normal circumstances. Although some citizens believed that the events taking place in Germany were wrong, Hitler's secret police used fear and force to wipe out potential criticism. After gaining almost complete control of the country, Hitler began conquering areas that he believed rightly belonged to Germany. This created tension throughout Europe that finally climaxed after his invasion of Poland with the British declaration of war on Germany and the start of the Second World War in Europe.

Ultranationalism also played a role in the onset of the Second World War in the Far East, as Japan's imperialist policies caused much tension around the world. The Japanese government envisioned a Japan with control throughout Asia and with unlimited access to the area's natural resources. Believing in Japan's entitlement to specific territory and having a need for resources, the country invaded areas in Asia. As a result, other countries, such as the United States, began to place restrictions on Japan's oil supplies, which further accelerated Japan's need for resources. This led to the attack on Pearl Harbor as the Japanese attempted to weaken American naval capabilities in the area in order to allow the Japanese to take over countries rich in oil. The United States retaliated and entered the Second World War. Once the war started, the war effort became part of every Japanese citizen's daily life, and those willing to sacrifice their lives for the cause were seen as brave heroes. Kamikaze fighters were fighter pilots who would deliberately crash their planes into allied targets in an effort to weaken the military or naval capabilities of Japan's enemies. These fighters were viewed as heroes, and the government's use of propaganda convinced many young Japanese men that this was an honourable thing to do for the country and Emperor.

During the war, many countries purposefully used their citizens' nationalistic sentiment to increase support for the war. Countries on both sides used poster and radio campaigns to gain support, both ideologically and economically, from their citizens. People were expected to sacrifice everyday items and in some countries, such as Great Britain, to endure rationing in order to support the war effort. Nationalism in Canada became more extreme when the government again began to single out groups it believed to be a threat to Canada's national security. After the attack on Pearl Harbor, some Canadians began to fear that those of Japanese ancestry living in British Columbia would begin to act as spies for the Japanese military. Racist policies, such as firing all Japanese Canadians who worked for the Canadian Pacific Railroad, began to be implemented. Japanese fishermen had their boats seized and were given very little or no compensation. In 1942, the Canadian government began to intern people of Japanese ancestry, even if they had been born in Canada. The internments took place primarily in British Columbia, although internment camps did exist in other parts of the country. Approximately 22 000 people were interned in total.

Practice Questions: 7 and 8

2.8 analyze ultranationalism as a cause of genocide (the Holocaust, 1932–1933 famine in Ukraine, contemporary examples)

Ultranationalism as a Cause of Genocide

At the present and throughout history, ultranationalism is and has been a cause of **genocide** (the intentional elimination of a group of people based on race, religion, ethnicity, or other cultural factors) and other human rights abuses. Often, ultranationalistic leaders use nationalism and pride in one's country as justification for their actions and racist policies. In the Soviet Union, ultranationalism led to the starvation deaths of millions of Ukrainians, referred to as the Ukrainian famine or *Holodomor*, as a result of Josef Stalin's agricultural policies. (Although some historians still debate whether the events of the *Holodomor* fall under the technical definition of genocide, the Ukrainian government and several other nations have officially recognized it as such.) In an effort to make the Soviet Union an economic powerhouse, Stalin introduced his Five Year Plans, which included strict collectivization of agriculture throughout the country. This meant that all farms were to be owned by the state and all profits made from them would go to the state. Although this policy applied to the whole country, it had the most disastrous effects in the region of the Ukraine from 1932 to 1933. Long considered the "bread basket" of the Soviet Union, this area produced more agricultural products, especially wheat, than any other area in the country, so its farms were heavily monitored. The people of the Ukraine were forced to give up virtually everything produced in the region, and as a result, people starved to death. The Soviet government set up check stops preventing people from leaving the area and imposed strict penalties, often death, upon people who attempted to keep or steal food. Stalin initiated a huge propaganda campaign depicting the people of the Ukraine as happy, healthy servants of the state to the rest of the country and the world.

Another historical example in which a sense of ultranationalism resulted in genocide is the Holocaust, which took place during the Second World War. As part of Adolf Hitler's plan to recreate glory for Germany, he used the Jewish population as a scapegoat for Germany's problems, including the loss of the First World War and the economic hardships that followed the war. He convinced much of the non-Jewish population that greatness for Germany could only come after the country was rid of Jews. He used propaganda to portray them as less than human, dirty, and untrustworthy. His systematic attempt to eliminate all Jews in Europe began quietly in Germany with the passing of the racist Nuremberg Laws, which took citizenship rights away from German Jews. Jews were terrorized by Hitler's *Schutzstaffel* (SS), and anyone considered to be sympathizing with the Jews was severely punished or murdered. Eventually, Jews were rounded up and put into ghettos in the cities and then "relocated" to work camps. During the war, Jews in any of the countries conquered by the Nazis fell victim to their policies. In 1942, Hitler initiated his Final Solution, which was the extermination of the Jewish population. Every day, thousands of Jewish people were murdered in death camps, such as the Auschwitz-Birkenau complex in Poland. Although exact numbers are hard to determine, approximately six million Jewish people were murdered during the Holocaust, and it is considered to be the worst case of genocide in recent history.

Contemporary examples of ultranationalism as a cause of genocide also exist. During the 1990s, the country of Yugoslavia experienced a series of wars when groups within the country began to demand independence. In an effort to preserve Serbia as the dominant republic in the area, Serbia's leader, Slobodan Milosevic, ordered the murder of thousands of Muslim people under the guise of "ethnic cleansing." Some of the worst atrocities took place during the war in Bosnia-Herzegovina and then in the province of Kosovo, where ethnic Albanians were being murdered. Milosevic believed that Serbia was historically entitled to much of the land in the area, and he did not want Serbs, who were minorities in some regions demanding independence, to be controlled by leaders of other ethnic groups. After extensive NATO and UN involvement, the wars in the region all ended by 1999. Milosevic eventually faced a war crimes tribunal at The Hague, where he died before his trial was completed.

Another contemporary example of genocide took place in the country of Rwanda on the continent of Africa in 1994. Here, much tension existed between two groups of people called the Hutus and Tutsis. Throughout the Belgian occupation of the country, the Tutsis (who were the minority) were favoured by the Belgians and enjoyed more privileges than the Hutus, which naturally angered the Hutus. After Rwanda gained independence in 1962, Hutu leaders were elected. Over the next years, these leaders employed prejudicial policies and engaged in persecution of the Tutsis. Both groups developed a sense of nationalism, as each felt victimized by the other, and this sense of nationalism, spurred along by propaganda, developed into hatred between members of the two groups, especially those considered to be "extremist." In 1994, when Hutu leader Juvénal Habyarimana's plane was shot down, the Hutus immediately blamed the Tutsis, although it remains unclear exactly who was responsible. This led to a 100-day bloodbath in which extremist Hutus brutally raped and murdered hundreds of thousands of Tutsis and moderate Hutus. Extreme Hutu nationalism was fuelled by propaganda, and between April and July, approximately 800 000 people were murdered. Hundreds of thousands more were maimed and more still were raped.

Practice Questions: 9 and 10

2.9 analyze impacts of the pursuit of national self-determination (successor states; decolonization; Québécois nationalism and sovereignty movement; First Nations, Métis and Inuit self-government; contemporary examples)

The Pursuit of National Self-Determination

National **self-determination** is the desire to have control over one's own nation or country without influence from other countries. This desire is usually held by a group of people who share a culture, language, and history. The pursuit of national self-determination in the past century has resulted in the birth of many new countries and the development of independent nations within countries. Successor states exist when a new state is created out of another. The successor state must uphold the international treaties and any human rights legislation adopted by the predecessor state. An example of a successor state is the Russian Federation, which was formed in 1991 after the dissolution of the Soviet Union. The majority of people of the Russian Federation share a common culture and language. Other independent countries were formed in regions of the former Soviet Union after the collapse of the country when the people of the dominant cultural group of those regions wished to govern themselves. However, these countries are not considered the successors of the Soviet Union.

Decolonization occurs when a country that has control over another country grants independence to it, severing political and economic control. The former colony gains sovereignty and assumes the responsibility of governing itself. Generally, decolonization refers to the period following the Second World War when European powers, who had at one time exercised extensive control in parts of Africa and Asia, granted independence to their former colonies. Many of these colonies had desired independence for a long time and had resented the control held over them by the colonist country. The colonies wished to have their borders drawn along cultural and geographic lines that reflected territory to which the colonist country believed it was entitled. An example of this situation occurred when India and Pakistan were created after Britain granted independence to British India in 1947. Although both India and Pakistan are sovereign countries, there continues to be dispute over the Kashmir region, parts of which are controlled by Pakistan, India, and China. Both Pakistan and India claim that they are rightly entitled to territories held by the others.

In Canada, national self-determination has been pursued by several different groups. Québécois nationalism and the sovereignty movement have led to various attempts at constitutional reform. Since the Quiet Revolution and the election of Jean Lesage as premier of Quebec in 1960, the sovereignty movement has been much more active than it had been formerly. The movement stems from the desire of some Quebecers to establish Quebec as a sovereign nation within Canada. It is primarily motivated by a belief that French culture in Quebec is unique from the rest of Canada, and in order to preserve it, Quebec must have more control over its affairs, both culturally and in representing itself on the international stage. Attempts to appease the concerns of Quebecers resulted in two failed attempts at persuading Quebec to endorse the Constitution patriated in 1982. The Meech Lake Accord and Charlottetown Accord both made attempts to recognize Quebec as a distinct society within Canada, but neither was successful. Quebec nationalism is fuelled by the belief that the Canadian government does not have Quebec's interests at heart and that the issues and concerns of French Canadians fall behind those of English Canadians. The separatist movement has also resulted in violence in Canada, particularly the Front de libération du Québec (FLQ) Crisis in October 1970. The FLQ was a terrorist organization that used the kidnapping and murder of government officials to make public their views and desires for a sovereign Quebec.

Other groups within Canada that desire national self-determination include First Nations people, the Métis, and the Inuit. Although each group has unique concerns and issues, all believe that members of their community are not properly served by the Canadian government and that they have a right to govern and make decisions for themselves because the government does not have an understanding of their unique culture and history. In this context, the term *self-government* is generally taken to include matters that affect the daily lives of people, such as education, language, culture, and economic development. The military, currency, and foreign relations are not included. Conflict over self-government exists between these groups and the Canadian government in regards to several issues; for example, how to prevent the laws of a self-governing group from contradicting those of the rest of the country, and pragmatic concerns such as how to organize the self-government within the Canadian constitution and government structure.

Practice Questions: 11 and 12

PRACTICE QUESTIONS—RELATED ISSUE 2

Use the following information to answer the next question.

Gavrilo Princip shot Archduke Franz Ferdinand in order to provoke a war between Austria and Serbia. Along with others, he hoped that such a war would ultimately result in Serbia's acquisition of Serbian lands in the Austrian Empire. The assassination was a means of rescuing national brothers who were stranded on the wrong side of the border between Austria and Serbia.

1. The given statement suggests the **main** motive for the assassination of Archduke Franz Ferdinand was to promote
   A. imperialistic goals
   B. militaristic desires
   C. nationalistic ambitions
   D. a campaign of revenge

2. According to the Department of National Defence, the **most important** goal of Canada's current National Defence Policy is to
   A. provide peacekeepers for UN missions
   B. push for the enlargement of the NATO alliance
   C. keep Canadians free from danger, harm, or threat
   D. dispose of landmines in war-torn areas of the globe

3. In deciding to adopt a policy of appeasement toward Fascist dictators, the British and French governments largely ignored the
   A. public wish that war must be avoided at any cost
   B. collective security apparatus of the League of Nations
   C. questionable military preparedness of their armed forces
   D. public feeling that certain territorial claims were justified

4. Evidence that the United States was not completely isolationist during the interwar period is **best** illustrated by American involvement in the
   A. Munich Pact
   B. Little Entente
   C. League of Nations
   D. Dawes and Young plans

Use the following information to answer the next question.

Characteristics of an Ultranationalistic State	
I	Difficult social and/or economic conditions
II	Tolerance of public dissent on government policies
III	Indoctrination of the country's youth
IV	Expectation for citizens to put the state ahead of themselves

5. Which of the given characteristics has been **incorrectly** included in the list?
   A. I
   B. II
   C. III
   D. IV

6. Which of the following types of governments is **most likely** to exist in an ultranationalistic country?
   A. Representative democracy
   B. Constitutional monarchy
   C. Direct democracy
   D. One-party system

7. Which of the following statements about the Battle of Vimy Ridge is **most accurate**?
   A. Canadian nationalism was non-existent before the battle.
   B. The battle was the first step taken by Canadians toward national independence from Britain.
   C. The battle advanced Canadian sovereignty but did little to create a national consciousness among Canadians.
   D. The battle created much stronger Canadian nationalism, which eventually led to Canadian sovereignty.

8. The **primary** motivation for the Japanese armed expansion in Asia that began in the early 1930s was to

   A. liberate Japanese people being ruled by brutal dictators

   B. restore good relations with both China and the United States

   C. make Japan the greatest economic and political power in Asia

   D. prevent the spread of communism in lands bordering the Soviet Union

Use the following information to answer the next question.

Nationalism is, by its very essence, dynamic rather than static. It is an explosive force, not a factor of stability.

9. The historical development that **best** supports the given contention is the

   A. turmoil in the Balkans during the 1990s

   B. absorption of Hong Kong into the People's Republic of China

   C. collapse of apartheid policies in South Africa during the 1990s

   D. agreement to include Poland, Hungary, and the Czech Republic in NATO

Use the following information to answer the next question.

From a Speech by Stalin in February, 1931

It is sometimes asked whether it is not possible to slow down the tempo somewhat, to put a check on the movement. No, comrades, it is not possible! The tempo must not be reduced!... To slacken the tempo would mean falling behind. And those who fall behind get beaten. No, we refuse to be beaten. ... We are 50 or 100 years behind the advanced countries. We must make good this distance in ten years. Either we do it, or we shall be crushed.

—from *Russia and the USSR: 1905–56*

10. In order to gain support for his policies, in this speech, Stalin appealed to which of the following feelings of Soviet citizens?

A. A belief that the only suitable leader to lead the Soviet Union to greatness was Josef Stalin

B. The desire for more freedom in the economy and for citizens to take part in the decision-making process

C. A belief in the ability to surpass the United States in the race for economic supremacy during the Cold War

D. The desire to make the Soviet Union a great country, recognized around the world for its achievements

11. During the 1980s and early 1990s, Quebec's politicians pushed for the recognition of Quebec within Canada's Constitution as a

A. sovereign state

B. distinct society

C. bilingual province

D. multicultural nation

12. During the Cold War, many nations achieved independence as a result of

A. decolonization in Africa and Asia

B. liberation movements in Latin America

C. struggles for power among ethnic groups in the Balkans

D. spheres of influence being established in the Middle East

ANSWERS AND SOLUTIONS—PRACTICE QUESTIONS

1. C	**4. D**	**7. D**	**10. D**
2. C	**5. B**	**8. C**	**11. B**
3. B	**6. D**	**9. A**	**12. A**

1. C

The given statement suggests the assassination of the archduke was motivated by the desire to unite all Serbs within the borders of a nation-state controlled by Serbia, which is a nationalistic desire.

The given statement does not suggest that revenge (the desire to inflict punishment for or avenge past wrongdoings), militarism (the build up and promotion of war), or imperialism (the desire to conquer and control foreign nations) were motives for the assassination of Archduke Ferdinand.

2. C

The top priority of Canada's (and any nation's) National Defence Policy is national security—that is, keeping members of the nation free from danger, harm, or threat.

Providing peacekeepers for UN missions, pushing for the enlargement of NATO alliances, and disposing of landmines in war-torn areas of the globe are all goals of Canada's National Defence Policy—but none of them is the top priority.

3. B

A policy of collective security is one in which countries agree to collectively guarantee the security of individual countries through sanctions or multilateral alliances against an aggressor; it is designed to preserve peace. Through their common membership in the League of Nations (a supranational organization for collective security), Britain, France, and Czechoslovakia pledged to defend one another from aggression. Rather than supporting Czechoslovakia by promising to defend it from attack by an aggressive Germany (as they had pledged to do according to the Covenant of the League of Nations), Britain and France chose to yield to the threats and demands of Germany. Britain and France allowed Germany to annex northwestern Czechoslovakia (the Sudetenland) rather than risk going to war with Germany over Czechoslovakia.

Appeasement was actually an attempt to satisfy strongly pacifistic British and French citizens. The Munich Agreement was very popular in Britain and France in 1938. Through this agreement, Britain and France appeased Hitler because they did not feel adequately prepared for a military confrontation with Nazi Germany. The British and French were also reluctant to go to war over the Sudetenland because they believed that this ethnically German region of Czechoslovakia rightly belonged to Germany.

4. D

Isolation is a policy of non-involvement in international affairs. The Dawes Plan (1924) and the Young Plan (1929) were two American-initiated schemes for reducing the burdens of Germany's war reparations payments. The United States' involvement in German and European affairs through these plans was a departure from America's interwar-era isolationism.

The United States did not participate in the Munich Pact, Little Entente, or League of Nations.

5. B

In an ultranationalistic state, there is little or no tolerance of dissent on government policies because citizens are expected to support the state regardless of their personal views. Those who outwardly express disagreement with the government are often severely punished.

The existence of difficult conditions, indoctrination, and the expectation for citizens to put the state ahead of the individual are all characteristics of an ultranationalistic state.

6. D

In an ultranationalistic state, the government is often controlled by one person or a ruling elite. The leaders in these countries rarely have competition and they may have policies in place to root out potential competition for power. In a representative democracy, citizens choose who they would like to represent them in government and that person is then accountable to the citizens. In a constitutional monarchy, there is an elected government that makes most decisions, as well as a monarch as the head of state who holds a mainly traditional role. In a direct democracy, each citizen has a say in all decisions made by government. Alternatives A, C, and B do not name types of governments that would likely exist in an ultranationalistic state.

7. D

Some historians claim that Canada became a nation on the day Canadian soldiers captured Vimy Ridge. What they mean by this is that Canadians first developed a strong national pride as a result of this spectacular military success. The stronger nationalism that emerged after the battle made Canadians more determined to end Canada's status as a mere colony of Great Britain. Canadians achieved this goal in 1931—only 14 years after the Battle of Vimy Ridge.

Canadian nationalism—albeit a relatively weak nationalism—existed prior to the battle. Canadians had taken other significant steps toward sovereignty before 1918—Confederation in 1867, for instance. The battle did a lot to create a Canadian national consciousness.

8. C

The main objective of Japanese expansionism in Asia during the 1930s and early 1940s was political and economic domination of Asia. At the time, Japan was an imperialist power attempting to create a huge Japanese empire in Asia. Japan sought direct political control of foreign nations, such as China, Vietnam, the Philippines, and Singapore. Japan also planned to exploit the natural resources of other Asian nations.

During the 1930 to 1945 era, Japan's foreign policy was not motivated by the desire to rescue mistreated Japanese nationals or to establish better relations with China and the United States. Although Japan signed the anti-communist Anti-Comintern Pact, expansionistic Japan wanted to increase the size of its own empire more than it wanted to stop the expansion of Russia's communist empire.

9. A

Ethnic nationalism ignited turmoil and instability in the Balkans (the mountainous area of southeastern Europe) during the 1990s. During this decade, Serbs fought several wars in an unsuccessful attempt to suppress nationalist independence movements in Slovenia, Croatia, Bosnia, and Kosovo.

Nationalism did not play much of a role in the collapse of the racist (anti-Black) policy of apartheid in South Africa, nor was it a factor in NATO's admission of Poland, Hungary, and the Czech Republic. Although China annexed Hong Kong for nationalist reasons (the Hong Kong people are part of the greater Chinese nation), this takeover was managed in a peaceful and orderly way.

10. D

In the quotation, Stalin is appealing to the feelings of nationalism held by Soviet citizens by suggesting they are strong and "refuse to be beaten" in order to gain support for his drastic economic policies.

The Cold War did not start until 1945, after the Second World War. Economic freedoms and citizen involvement in decision making are not addressed in the quotation. Although Stalin used extensive propaganda to encourage the belief among Soviet citizens that he was the only suitable leader for the Soviet Union, this is not the topic of the quotation in the source.

11. B

Liberal governments in Quebec in the 1980s and 1990s pushed for recognition of Quebec as a "distinct society," especially in the Meech Lake and Charlottetown accords.

Although Parti Québécois governments have pushed for Quebec sovereignty, they have never pursued recognition of Quebec's independence in the Canadian Constitution. After all, no nation's constitution recognizes the sovereignty of another sovereign country. Quebec separatists ultimately wanted to create a new constitution for an independent Quebec. In the 1980s and 1990s, virtually all provincial politicians in Quebec opposed the policies of bilingualism and multiculturalism. They pursued policies of unilingualism within Quebec and preferred the old model of biculturalism over the new model of multiculturalism.

12. A

During the 1945 to 1991 era, many European colonies in Africa and Asia gained political independence.

Latin America underwent decolonization in the nineteenth century. Nations in the Balkans (southeastern Europe) gained national sovereignty prior to the First World War or during the 1990s. The establishment of a sphere of influence is a form of imperialism that erodes national sovereignty.

UNIT TEST—RELATED ISSUE 2

Use the following information to answer the next two questions.

Developments in Great Britain During the Interwar Years, 1919 to 1939

- Strong pacifist movements opposed involvement in European affairs.
- Many British leaders felt that the peace treaties following the First World War dealt too harshly with the defeated powers.
- The economic disaster of the Great Depression led to large cuts in military spending.
- Public opinion was strongly against military confrontation.

1. These developments encouraged the British government to adopt a foreign policy of

A. appeasing Fascist demands

B. deterring Communist expansion

C. supporting American isolationism

D. withdrawing from continental affairs

2. The given developments created a climate that fostered public support for Great Britain's signing of the

A. Balfour Declaration

B. Treaty of Versailles

C. Yalta Agreement

D. Munich Accord

3. The popular appeal of fascism in both Italy and Germany during the interwar years can be attributed largely to the emphasis that Fascist ideology placed on

A. racial discrimination

B. ultranationalistic fervour

C. isolationist foreign policies

D. class struggle between rich and poor

Use the following information to answer the next three questions.

Source I

The most aggressive nationalists in the Balkans were the Serbs. The kingdom of Serbia had been set up late in the previous century when its people had fought for independence from the decaying Turkish Empire. But that was not enough for Serbian nationalists: they planned to create a Yugoslavia (South Slavia) by joining all the Slav peoples who lived in the southern part of the Austrian Empire. To Vienna, this would mean the end of their empire: if the Southern Slavs were allowed to break away, it would only be a matter of time before the Czechs, Poles, Hungarians, and Slovaks went their separate ways as well.

— from *Twentieth Century History: The World Since 1900*

Source II

Yugoslavian Nationalists

Source III

Yugoslavia might survive as an entity in international law. This Yugoslavia would consist of a loose confederation of six sovereign nation-states.... It is assumed that Serbia, Montenegro, Bosnia and Herzegovina, and Macedonia would remain within Yugoslavia. The most important disputed issue in this case would be that of Serbian people living in Croatia, who have declared that they would refuse to remain within an independent Croatian state. Furthermore, Serbia is willing to accept only a solution that enables all Serbs to live in one state. Thus, this option could be translated into reality by peaceful means only with difficulty and might well become a reason for civil war in Yugoslavia.... Finally, the armed forces, strictly observing the country's constitution, might seize power to prevent the disintegration of Yugoslavia.

— from *World Press Review, 1991*

4. Which of the following statements presents the **main** generalization inherent in the three given sources?

A. Aggressive nationalism is a destabilizing force.

B. Self-determination is a catalyst in solving ethnic conflict.

C. Ethnic divisions can be resolved through the United Nations.

D. Superpower intervention can no longer prevent boundary disputes.

5. In addition to the problem caused by the death of Marshall Tito, the problems depicted in Source II and Source III were intensified by the

A. interference of UN peacekeeping forces

B. disintegration of the former Soviet Bloc

C. threatened use of force by the superpowers

D. strong diplomacy of the Western European powers

6. Given subsequent events, the writer of Source III, commenting in 1991, was quite correct in observing that

A. "Yugoslavia would consist of a loose confederation of six sovereign nation-states"

B. "Serbia is willing to accept only a solution that enables all Serbs to live in one state"

C. "all Serbs [living] in one state … might well become a reason for civil war"

D. "the armed forces … might seize power to prevent the disintegration of Yugoslavia"

Use the following information to answer the next question.

> The Republican party maintains the traditional American policy of non-interference in the political affairs of other nations. This government has definitely refused membership in the League of Nations and to assume any obligations under the covenant of the League. On this we stand.
>
> —Republican National Platform, 1928
>
> —from *Internationalism: Opposing Viewpoints*

7. The given declaration was made during a time when the United States pursued a foreign policy of

A. isolationism

B. expansionism

C. interventionism

D. internationalism

8. In the 1920s and 1930s, one factor that united members of the Nazi party was their shared resentment of

A. German ex-soldiers who used violence to create social unrest

B. German nationalists who idealized Germany's past glories

C. the ideals and goals of Fascist politicians

D. the terms of the Treaty of Versailles

Use the following quotation to answer the next question.

> The Germans, if this government is elected, are going to pay every penny; they are going to be squeezed, as a lemon is squeezed, until the pips squeak.
>
> —A British politician, December 9, 1918
>
> —from *The Twentieth Century World*

9. The given quotation provides information highlighting the political climate that existed during the creation of the

A. terms of the Munich Pact

B. the United Nations Charter

C. terms of the Treaty of Versailles

D. Covenant of the League of Nations

Use the following information to answer the next two questions.

> **Night of Terror in Germany 1938**
>
> The Jewish community in Germany endured a night of terror when Nazi thugs went on the rampage, attacking Jewish businesses, synagogues and property. Thirty-six people were killed during the night, and 20 000 arrested; more than 7 000 shops were looted and 267 synagogues burnt down. Dr. Goebbels, Minister of Public Enlightenment and Propaganda, claimed that the violence was a "spontaneous reaction" to the assassination in Paris of Ernst von Rath, a German diplomat, by a young Polish Jew. There is no doubt, however, that the pogrom was carried out on the instructions of the Gestapo. A chilling development was the involvement of the "respectable" middle classes; fashionable women clapped as Jews were beaten by youths wielding lead piping. So that the insurance companies are not bankrupted by state hooliganism, the Nazis have declared their intention to confiscate insurance payouts and return them to the insurers. The huge amount of glass broken has led to the night being dubbed "Kristallnacht"; replacement glass will have to be imported and paid for in foreign currency. "They should have killed more Jews and broken less glass," grumbled Hermann Goering.
>
> —from *On This Day*

10. The writer suggests that the attack on German Jews was

A. a sudden event that angered Nazi leaders

B. organized by representatives of foreign governments

C. directed by representatives of the German government

D. an event that had been expected by many for some time

11. A technique of dictatorship demonstrated by the given event is the

A. scapegoating of a minority group

B. use of propaganda to unite all citizens

C. promotion of tolerance for cultural differences

D. encouraging of people to participate in the political process

12. Which of the following terms is used to describe the dramatic transformation of Quebec's cultural and political attitudes that occurred during the 1960s?
   A. The Conquest
   B. The FLQ Crisis
   C. The Duplessis Era
   D. The Quiet Revolution

Use the following information to answer the next two questions.

> If we had tried to identify each of the minorities in Canada in order to protect all of the characteristics that made them different, not only would we have been faced with an impossible task, but we would shortly have been presiding over the balkanization of Canada. The danger inherent in this would have been particularly acute in the case of minorities that are in a position to be identified with a given territory, like the Celts in Nova Scotia, the Acadians in New Brunswick, the French Canadians in Quebec, and the Indians and Inuit in the Far North.
>
> —Pierre Trudeau, 1992

13. In his use of the phrase "the balkanization of Canada," Trudeau is referring to
   A. the break up of Canada into smaller states
   B. an uncontrollable tide of immigration to Canada
   C. an end to Canada's official policy of multiculturalism
   D. the granting of special rights to Canada's minority groups

14. Based on the views he expressed in the given quotation, which one of the following actions would Trudeau **most likely** have opposed?
   A. The creation of the new territory of Nunavut
   B. The settlement of longstanding Aboriginal land claims
   C. The inclusion of several French Canadians in the federal cabinet
   D. Federal government funding for multicultural festivals such as Edmonton's Heritage Days or Winnipeg's Folklorama

Use the following information to answer the next two questions.

Some Authoritarian Actions Taken by the Canadian Government in the Twentieth Century	
Action I	Censorship
Action II	Conscription
Action III	Suspension of civil liberties
Action IV	Internment of enemy aliens
Action V	Invoking of the War Measures Act

15. The Canadian government's use of the given actions during the twentieth century **most clearly** suggests that during times of national threat, it is

A. acceptable to suspend the rights of aliens and foreign nationals

B. essential that potential traitors be monitored by the government

C. unwise for a government to give priority to the protection of civil rights

D. difficult for a democracy to respect individual rights while fighting a war

16. Which two of the given actions caused the **greatest** harm to Canadian national unity during the twentieth century?

A. Actions I and IV

B. Actions II and V

C. Actions III and IV

D. Actions IV and V

Use the following information to answer the next question.

During times of severe hardship, political parties that were once considered too extreme may come to enjoy widespread voter support.

17. The given statement is **best** supported by the actions of the

A. National Socialist party in Germany during the 1930s

B. Communist party in the Soviet Union during the 1960s

C. Democratic party in the United States during the 1980s

D. Progressive Conservative party in Canada during the 1990s

18. The **primary** motivation behind the eagerness of European nations to go to war in 1914 was their common national interests in
   A. militarism
   B. irredentism
   C. imperialism
   D. isolationism

19. All of the following actions are more closely associated with ultranationalistic states rather with nationalistic states **except**
   A. imprisonment of those deemed unsupportive of government policies
   B. state-supported centennial celebrations, such as a national holiday
   C. the use of a scapegoat to legitimize extreme government policies
   D. censorship of school texts to misrepresent a country's history

20. The pursuit of national interest by a democratic government is **most often** fuelled by
   A. a leader's hopes to acquire complete decision-making authority in the country
   B. a government's desire to achieve the best possible standing for its country
   C. an attempt to promote feelings of internationalism among countries
   D. a desire to appease or placate the concerns of its allies

ANSWERS AND SOLUTIONS—UNIT TEST

1. A	**5. B**	**9. C**	**13. A**	**17. A**
2. D	**6. C**	**10. C**	**14. A**	**18. A**
3. B	**7. A**	**11. A**	**15. D**	**19. B**
4. A	**8. D**	**12. D**	**16. B**	**20. B**

1. A

The given developments encouraged Britain to adopt a foreign policy of appeasement (giving in to an aggressor-nation in an effort to placate it and thereby avoid a confrontation). A strong pacifist movement in Britain, among other things, made Britain reluctant to confront Germany or Italy during the 1930s. Instead, Britain sought to appease the Fascist powers through the Hoare–Laval Pact and the Munich Pact.

The given developments did not change Britain's relations with the Soviet Union. They did not lead Britain to support American isolationism (non-participation in international affairs) or to withdraw from continental (European) affairs.

2. D

These developments created a climate of support for appeasement that resulted in the Munich Accord (the 1938 agreement in which Germany was given the Sudetenland in Czechoslovakia in return for the assurance that Hitler would not seek to annex or invade other European territories).

The given developments had no impact on public support for the 1919 Treaty of Versailles (peace treaty between Germany and the Allied Powers), the 1917 Balfour Declaration (a British statement of support for a Jewish homeland in Palestine), or the 1945 Yalta Agreement (the deal struck by Stalin, Roosevelt, and Churchill at a summit meeting during the Second World War).

3. B

The Fascists used nationalism to attract the support of the intensely nationalistic Germans and Italians. The Germans were impressed by the extreme nationalistic fervour (ultranationalism) that was on display at every Fascist rally and ceremony.

Racism was not a major ingredient of Italian fascism and, even in Germany, ultranationalism gained the Fascists more supporters than did their racial policies. Neither Italian Fascists nor German Fascists embraced isolationism (non-participation in alliances or in the affairs of other states); Mussolini's Italy and Nazi Germany both entered into alliances and intervened in the affairs of other states—in the Spanish Civil War, for example. Finally, both German and Italian Fascists promoted nationalism as the ultimate remedy for class divisions: Fascists, unlike Communists, do not encourage the class struggle between rich and poor; Fascists encourage both rich and poor members of the nation to see each other as national brothers. Fascists see the world as an arena for the struggle between nations, not classes.

4. A

All of the sources point to aggressive nationalism as a destabilizing force. Serbian nationalism was one of the key causes of the First World War.

In the case of Yugoslavia, self-determination (the right of a people to govern themselves as a nation) has led to ethnic conflict as the various ethnic groups in the country have broken away. There are very few examples of the United Nations successfully determining ethnic divisions. Most ethnic divisions in this century have been determined by force, not diplomacy. The statement in alternative D may well be true, but there is no reference to it in any of the sources.

5. B

The threat posed by the Soviet Union acted as a unifying force on Yugoslavia. With the collapse of Soviet power and the end of the Cold War, this unifying factor was removed.

The United Nations attempted, with limited success, to halt the ethnic strife that erupted between the Serbs and the various other ethnic groups that had once comprised a united Yugoslavia. The United Nations did nothing to intensify the problems created by the break up of Yugoslavia, but sought rather to establish a peaceful solution to the problem. Only the United States threatened force against Yugoslavia and then only against breakaway ethnic groups that carried out violent acts. Diplomatic efforts by Western powers were aimed at restoring some semblance of stability in the Balkans, not encouraging a further breakup of Yugoslavia.

6. C

In states with a Serb minority, violent clashes occurred between members of the new states and the Serb minorities. This violence was supported by the Yugoslavian army. Over 200 000 people died in ethnic violence.

The former Yugoslavia has broken into five separate sovereign states. At the time this question was administered, a sixth state, Kosovo, was attempting to assert its independence. Although the Serbs attempted to unite all territories with Serbian populations, it has been forced to accept that some Serbs will have to live as minorities in some of the breakaway states. The Yugoslavian military has not attempted to seize power in what is left of Yugoslavia.

7. A

In 1919–20, after refusing to ratify (approve) the Treaty of Versailles and deciding not to join the League of Nations, the United States adopted a foreign policy of isolationism. A policy of isolationism stresses that peace and economic advancement can best be achieved by isolating one's country from alliances with and commitments to other nations.

During the interwar period, the United States did not embrace a foreign policy of expansionism (expanding one's national territory by conquest and/or annexation), interventionism (active involvement or interference in the internal affairs of other countries), or internationalism (working for the general benefit of the human race).

8. D

Members of the Nazi party hated the terms of the Treaty of Versailles, as did most Germans. Hitler's popularity among Germans stemmed partly from his repeated condemnations of the treaty.

Many Nazis were ex-soldiers who used violence to create social unrest. All Nazis were reactionary nationalists who had an idealized view of Germany's history. All Nazi party members were Fascists who followed a Fascist political leader (Adolf Hitler).

9. C

The Treaty of Versailles was imposed upon Germany in 1919 by the victorious Allies after the First World War. The Allies designed the treaty in such a way that Germany had to make reparations for the war.

The Munich Pact was signed by Britain, France, Germany, and Italy in 1938. This agreement ceded the Sudetenland to Germany. The United Nations Charter (1945) and the Covenant of the League of Nations (1919) were the agreements that laid out the beliefs and policies of each of those organizations. Neither agreement included collecting monetary payments from Germany.

10. C

The writer suggests the attack on German Jews was directed by representatives of the German government. He states, "There is no doubt… that the pogrom was carried out on the instructions of the Gestapo." (A pogrom is an organized massacre or persecution, especially of Jewish people.) The Gestapo was the German secret police force that was directed first by Herman Goering and later by Heinrich Himmler—the most powerful government officials in Nazi Germany after Hitler himself.

The writer suggests that Kristallnacht was an event planned by the Nazi government and that it greatly pleased Nazi leaders. He does not maintain that foreign governments organized the event or that the event had been expected for some time.

11. A

The events of Kristallnacht provide a good example of the scapegoating of a minority group. The government of Nazi Germany blamed one Jewish man's actions on all the Jews and directed popular discontent against them. The Nazis' scapegoating of the Jews was so successful that even "fashionable women clapped as Jews were beaten by youths."

Kristallnacht was more than just a propaganda event—it involved large-scale organized violence against a minority group. Furthermore, the event did not promote tolerance (acceptance) of cultural differences; rather, it involved the persecution of a minority group with a different culture. This event did not encourage people to participate in the political process—the event was planned, directed, and controlled by Germany's dictatorial government, not ordinary people.

12. D

The dramatic transformation of Quebec's culture, government, and society during the 1960s is known as the Quiet Revolution.

The Conquest refers to the British use of military force to overcome and control New France (Quebec) in 1759–1760. Through the Conquest, Quebec ceased to be a colony of France and became a British colony.
The FLQ Crisis (October Crisis) occurred in Quebec in 1970. It was a struggle between the government and Québécois separatist terrorists from the Front de libération du Québec (FLQ). The Duplessis Era refers to the tenure of Quebec's authoritarian provincial premier, Maurice Duplessis, who was in power in Quebec during most of the 1936–59 period. The Quiet Revolution was, in part, a rebellion against the ultraconservative economic, social, and political system established and maintained by Duplessis.

13. A

***Balkanization* refers to "the process of dividing a country into smaller, mutually hostile states."**

An uncontrollable tide of immigrants to Canada, an end to Canada's official policy of multiculturalism, and the granting of special rights to Canada's minorities do not match the definition of *balkanization*.

14. A

Based on his statement, Trudeau would most likely have opposed the creation of Nunavut. He states that it would be unwise to give political power to "minorities that are in a position to be identified with a given territory." Canada, in giving territorial status to a region inhabited almost exclusively by the Inuit people, evidently ignored Trudeau's advice.

Nothing in Trudeau's statement suggests that he opposed the settlement of longstanding Aboriginal land claims, the inclusion of French Canadians in the federal cabinet, or federal government funding for multicultural festivals.

15. D

The five given actions indicate that it is difficult for a democracy to respect individual rights while fighting a war. In both World Wars, Canada set aside or violated basic civil liberties.

The five given actions do not support the idea that it is acceptable to suspend the rights of aliens and foreign nationals, essential that potential traitors be monitored by the government, or unwise for a government to give priority to the protection of civil rights.

16. B

Implementing conscription (during both World Wars) and the invoking of the War Measures Act in 1970 (during the October Crisis) greatly damaged the relationship between Quebec and the rest of Canada.

Censorship, the suspension of civil liberties, and the internment of enemy aliens did not cause as much harm as did conscription and invoking the War Measures Act.

17. A

The National Socialist party gained popular support in Germany during the early 1930s when the country was experiencing a severe economic depression that Germany's mainstream political parties seemed unable to reverse. Nazism attracted voters through Hitler's bold promises to eliminate unemployment and revive Germany's economic power.

While the Soviet Communist party may be considered extreme, it was already in power in the 1960s and the country was not experiencing severe hardship at that time. The Democratic party in the United States and the Progressive Conservative party in Canada are both mainstream parties, not extremist (ultra-left or ultra-right) parties.

18. A

Militarism is the love of war and military conquest. The great enthusiasm for war in the summer of 1914 was a potent mixture of militarism and ultranationalism.

The great enthusiasm expressed by most combatant nations in 1914 cannot be adequately explained by imperialism (support for the expansion of empires) or irredentism (the desire to annex adjacent territories that contain members of one's nationality). Not all of the nations sought goals of imperialist expansion or irredentism at the outbreak of the First World War. If nations had been motivated by isolationism (the desire to avoid foreign entanglements), they would not have been eager to go to war.

19. B

Many countries that are considered nationalistic have governments that support country-wide celebrations of milestones, such as a country's centennial or the yearly anniversary of the country's nationhood.

Imprisonment of dissidents, the use of a scapegoat, and censorship are actions that would more likely be taken by an ultranationalistic government than a nationalistic government.

20. B

The pursuit of national interest by a democratic government is most often an attempt to make conditions optimal for the country, both domestically and internationally.

Most democratic countries do not have leaders who are attempting to gain complete decision-making authority. Internationalism is the concern for the well-being of other nations, which is not the goal of a country pursing its national interests. Appeasing or placating concerns of other countries is not a priority when pursuing national interests.

Related Issue 3

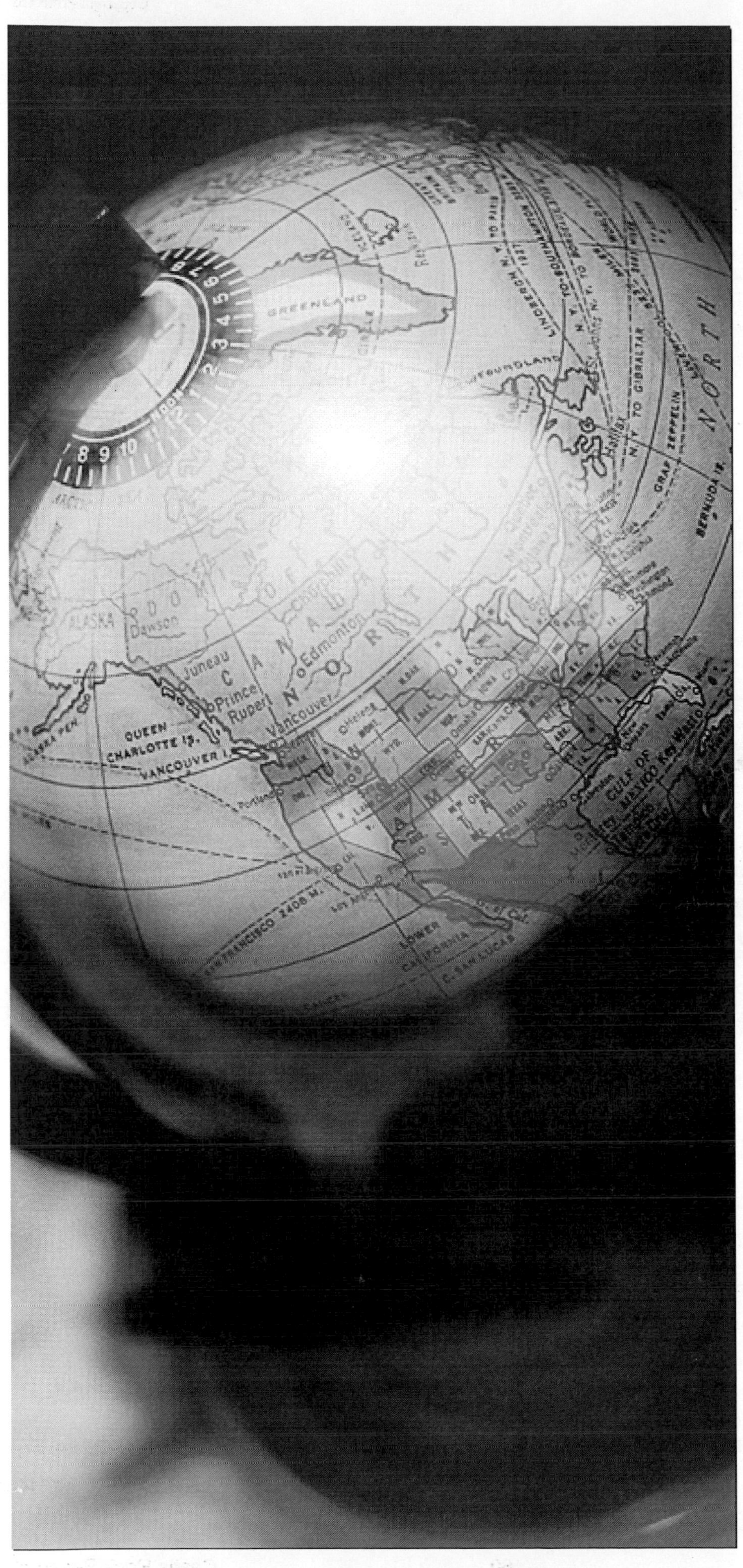

RELATED ISSUE 3

Table of Correlations

Specific Outcome	Practice Questions	Unit Test Questions	Practice Test 1	Practice Test 2
Students will assess impacts of the pursuit of internationalism in contemporary global affairs.				
3.4 analyze the motives of nation and state involvement or noninvolvement in international affairs (economic stability, self-determination, peace, security, humanitarianism)	1, 2	1, 3, 10, 15	4, 10, 12	3, 4, 9, 10
3.5 explore understandings of internationalism	3, 4	5, 8, 14	11, 16	1, 26, 42
3.6 analyze how internationalism can be promoted through foreign policy (multilateralism, supranationalism, peacekeeping, foreign aid, international law and agreements)	5, 6	2, 4, 9, 12	13	6
3.7 evaluate the extent to which selected organizations promote internationalism (United Nations, World Council of Indigenous Peoples, European Union, l'Organisation internationale de la Francophonie, Arctic Council, contemporary examples)	7, 8	6, 7, 13, 18, 19, 20	8, 14, 15, 23, 25	2
3.8 analyze impacts of the pursuit of internationalism in addressing contemporary global issues (conflict, poverty, debt, disease, environment, human rights)	9	11, 17	24	27
3.9 evaluate the extent to which nationalism must be sacrificed in the interest of internationalism	10, 11	16	9	5, 43

RELATED ISSUE 3

To What Extent Should Internationalism be Pursued?

Internationalism – the belief in the importance of cooperation among countries in order to promote the common good for all countries in both social and economic terms.

3.4 analyze the motives of nation and state involvement or noninvolvement in international affairs (economic stability, self-determination, peace, security, humanitarianism)

Nation and State Involvement in International Affairs

The involvement or noninvolvement of a nation or nation-state in international affairs can be motivated by many factors. Generally, governments choose to become involved in international affairs if they believe there is some benefit for their country in addition to a possible global benefit. A major factor in such a decision is economic stability. In order to expand their economy or maintain their competitiveness on a global scale, countries may choose to involve themselves in international economic discussions, organizations, or alliances. Examples of these are the G8, NAFTA, and the EU, among many others. The G8 (Group of Eight) is an organization of eight of the wealthiest countries in the world. They meet to discuss global matters, often related to economics and the promotion of the global economy. NAFTA (North American Free Trade Agreement) is an alliance in which its members (Canada, the United States, and Mexico) have agreed to make the flow of goods across each others' borders easier by reducing tariffs and other trade barriers. The hope of such an alliance is that each of the economies involved will benefit from larger markets, more competition, and increased availability of goods. The EU (European Union) is a group of European countries that have removed many trade barriers and introduced a common currency, and that, together, work to promote the European economy on the global market.

Just as countries may see a benefit of becoming involved in international affairs for economic stability, noninvolvement may also been seen as beneficial, and countries may choose a more isolationist perspective in order to promote their own economies. They may introduce policies, such as tariffs, that further separate them from other economies.

Another motivation for involvement or noninvolvement in international affairs is self-determination, which is the desire for a group of people with common culture, history, and language to have control over their own country. Nations that desire self-determination may seek involvement in international affairs in order to gain the support of the international community for their declaration of independence. They may seek to prove their ability to compete in the global economy or as a military force on the international stage.

The pursuit of peace and security are also motivations for countries to either become more involved in or more isolated from international affairs. By securing alliances with other countries, a country may guarantee protection or support in the event of a conflict. Many countries believe that such alliances promote international security. They believe that hostile countries are less likely to threaten them with military action because they have the military support of all the other countries in the alliance. NATO and the former Warsaw Pact are examples of such alliances. NATO (North Atlantic Treaty Organization) was formed after the Second World War to protect Western Europe and North America from the perceived Soviet threat. In response, the Soviet Union initiated the Warsaw Pact with its satellite countries in order to protect against the perceived NATO threat. Both alliances lasted through the Cold War, during which there were no direct conflicts between the superpowers involved in each alliance. A buildup of alliances also occurred in the early twentieth century, as countries hoped to protect themselves against aggressive empires, particularly in Europe. Some countries choose to become involved in international organizations such as the United Nations, which works to promote international peace and stability. In addition, conferences and agreements may be held among several nations in an attempt to promote peace and security. For example, during the Cold War, various agreements such as SALT (Strategic Arms Limitations Treaty) I and II were made in an effort to slow the production and spread of nuclear weapons.

Countries may also choose involvement in international affairs for humanitarian reasons. For example, if there is an abuse of human rights in a particular country, others may choose to take actions, such as sanctions or international condemnation, to try to force change in the country. Countries may even take collective military action to stop human rights abuses within a sovereign country. The point at which the international community has a responsibility to do this is often a topic of debate at international discussions, such as those held by the United Nations. Involvement in international affairs for humanitarian reasons can also occur as a result of events such as a natural disaster or civil war. Countries may send aid, such as food or medicine, to people in need. Sometimes, such involvement is motivated by a potential benefit for the country providing the aid, which may receive economic rewards for the aid it supplies.

Practice Questions: 1 and 2

3.5 explore understandings of internationalism

INTERNATIONALISM

Internationalism is an ideology that centres on the idea that cooperation among countries will improve the overall standing of each country involved, more than if each country chose to put its own issues and concerns ahead of such cooperation. Internationalism focuses primarily on economic and political issues, but social conditions and the promotion of culture can also be priorities. Opposition to internationalism usually arises out of the premise that a country cannot be concerned both with its own best interests as well as those of others. However, as more attempts are made at international cooperation in modern times, many are starting to believe that a country that supports internationalism does not necessarily have to abandon nationalism—countries can be patriotic and nationalistic while still maintaining an internationalist perspective.

Practice Questions: 3 and 4

3.6 analyze how internationalism can be promoted through foreign policy (multilateralism, supranationalism, peacekeeping, foreign aid, international law and agreements)

The Promotion of Internationalism Through Foreign Policy

A country's commitment to internationalism and its willingness to participate in international affairs are reflected in its foreign policy. A country's foreign policy involves the decisions made by its government as to how the country will participate in issues, agreements, or conflicts worldwide. Multilateral agreements (those involving more than two countries) can include political, military, or economic alliances. Multilateral actions, which may be aggressive or peaceful in nature, often serve to promote the ideology of internationalism.

Supranationalism is a type of decision-making in which countries have representatives in an organization and the organization is able to make decisions for the group as a whole. Countries may still be independent, but some of their decision-making power has been surrendered to the larger group. When countries choose to become involved in multilateral agreements or supranationalistic organizations, they are promoting internationalism through foreign policy. Internationalism can also be promoted through a country's willingness to become involved in affairs outside of its own borders, even if such involvement may have detrimental results for the country. For example, sometimes countries send military personnel to regions experiencing conflict in an effort to maintain a fragile peace or to put an end to aggression. Through this involvement in peacekeeping, a country is attempting to improve the well-being of citizens in another country, even if it means losing the lives of its own military personnel and expending significant funds to support the mission.

A country can also promote internationalism by adopting a foreign policy of providing foreign aid to other countries that are experiencing economic, social, or political difficulties. Aid may be required for many reasons, such as civil war or natural disasters, and can be provided in various forms, such as monetary, medical, or manpower. Sometimes, countries provide "tied aid," which means that the country providing aid expects some kind of benefit in exchange. For example, a country may provide the funds and materials to build a hospital but then require that all supplies and drugs be purchased from businesses in the country that provided the aid. Similarly, a country may provide aid and expect support for political policies or military action in return.

Countries sometimes sign international laws or agreements in order to promote internationalism. These laws or agreements may include those related to environmental issues such as the Kyoto Protocol or the United Nations Climate Change Conference, which took place in Bali in December 2007. Economic agreements, such as those made by the World Trade Organization, or agreements related to social conditions, which are often spearheaded by the United Nations, are also ways in which countries can promote internationalism.

Practice Questions: 5 and 6

3.7 evaluate the extent to which selected organizations promote internationalism (United Nations, World Council of Indigenous Peoples, European Union, l'Organisation internationale de la Francophonie, Arctic Council, contemporary examples)

The Extent to Which Organizations Promote Internationalism

There are various organizations around the world that work to promote internationalism. A good example of one of these organizations is the **United Nations** (UN). The UN is an organization, with 192 member-countries, that works to promote peace and security around the world. Two of the main bodies of the UN are the **General Assembly** and the **Security Council**. The General Assembly meets to discuss issues of worldwide importance that range from economic to humanitarian to social to environmental. In the General Assembly, each country has one seat and one vote. The Security Council is comprised of five permanent members (Russia, China, France, the United States, and the United Kingdom) as well as ten non-permanent members that rotate on a two-year basis. The Security Council's main job is to decide if, when, and how the UN will become involved in conflict around the world. The General Assembly may make recommendations to the Security Council; however, the Council is not obliged to follow or implement these recommendations. The United Nations has many other bodies that work toward various goals, some of which include stopping the spread of HIV/AIDS, eradicating poverty, improving the status of women and children, and ensuring environmental sustainability. Through membership in the United Nations, countries demonstrate a willingness to promote and participate in internationalism.

The **World Council of Indigenous Peoples** (WCIP) was an organization that existed from 1975 to 1996 and that worked to promote the rights of indigenous peoples around the world. Key issues for the organization included land claims, self-government, social justice, the preservation of indigenous cultures, and the economic prosperity of indigenous peoples.

The **European Union** (EU) is a community of 27 European nations that works to promote peace and economic stability among its members. The organization has gone through several stages and has had several names, including the European Economic Community and the European Common Market. It had its start following the Second World War when European countries wanted to make sure that the destruction of the war would not happen again. Countries within the EU maintain their sovereignty but willingly allow some decisions that affect all members to be made democratically within the EU. The euro is the common currency used by 13 of the member countries, and when the economies of the remaining members are strong enough (or, as in the case of the United Kingdom, they choose to adopt it), they will also use the euro. Citizens are not required to carry passports to travel between member countries. Efforts have been made to reduce or eliminate trade barriers between member countries to allow for economic growth and for the EU to compete more effectively in the international economy. The EU also works to promote human rights and environmental issues within its member countries and around the world.

L'Organisation internationale de la Francophonie (OIF) is an organization of 55 countries and 13 observer countries in which the French language is prevalent and part of the country's history. The OIF works primarily to promote French as an international language and to promote cultural diversity worldwide. In addition, the OIF works to promote democracy and human rights, both within its members and worldwide.

The **Arctic Council** is a forum consisting of eight member countries and permanent participants representing groups of indigenous peoples living in the Arctic. The council works to promote cooperation among member states and participants, particularly regarding issues of the environment and economic sustainability.

A contemporary example of an organization that promotes internationalism is Amnesty International (AI). This nongovernmental group works to highlight human rights abuses around the world and uses public pressure to influence the release or improved treatment of political prisoners. In addition, Amnesty International encourages citizens of countries that are generally considered to have strong human rights records to lobby their governments to use political and economic pressure against countries in which human rights abuses are occurring.

Practice Questions: 7 and 8

3.8 analyze impacts of the pursuit of internationalism in addressing contemporary global issues (conflict, poverty, debt, disease, environment, human rights)

The Pursuit of Internationalism

The pursuit of internationalism can have an impact on global issues as countries work together to address these issues or as countries ignore these issues in an effort to maintain political or economic alliances. When conflicts arise, countries will often work together through organizations such as the United Nations to put a stop to the conflict. Countries may impose sanctions or, in some cases, authorize the use of force through an international group of military forces. In some cases, countries have been accused of abandoning their commitments to internationalism when they are unwilling to address or provide military support in a conflict.

Internationalism can have an impact on poverty and debt in countries. The more integrated the world's economy becomes, the more difficult it is for developing countries to compete on the international market. As a result, many developing countries have incurred crippling debts. Governments of poverty-stricken countries sometimes try to lure multinational corporations with the promise of few or no labour laws. Impoverished nations sometimes have to borrow large amounts of money to sustain the country, but then they enter into a cycle of borrowing more money to try to pay back their debts and the interest on those debts. Efforts have been made to relieve the debt repayment of developing countries, and organizations such as the United Nations work to reduce poverty through education and empowerment programs. With support from other countries, organizations such as the International Monetary Fund and the World Bank also work to address issues of debt and poverty in developing countries.

Another area in which efforts of internationalism can have an effect is the area of human rights. Many international organizations have made the protection of human rights part of their mandate, even if that is not the primary focus of their organization. Countries can use political and economic pressure to effect policy changes in countries where human rights are being abused. Documents such as the Universal Declaration of Human Rights set a standard to which all the countries of the world are to adhere. When several countries do this together, the pressure has even more effect. As well, nongovernmental organizations such as Amnesty International work to raise awareness of issues like human rights on a global scale.

Countries sometimes work together to address issues, such as health (e.g., disease) or the environment, that affect all countries of the world. For example, several organizations, including the G8 and UN, have introduced programs to slow the spread of AIDS and secure funding for efforts to find a cure. Countries are working together to address issues such as global warming through international agreements like the Kyoto Protocol and summits such as the Bali Climate Summit. All countries in the world have a reason to embrace internationalism in an effort to find solutions because all countries in the world would benefit from such solutions.

Practice Question: 9

3.9 evaluate the extent to which nationalism must be sacrificed in the interest of internationalism

Nationalism versus Internationalism

To some extent, nationalism must be sacrificed in the interest of internationalism as countries must balance their own requirements or desires with the best interest of the international community. If governments are committed to internationalism, they must consider global issues and how policies made within their countries could potentially impact other nations.

Being a member of an international organization can also mean sacrificing some sovereignty in order to support the goals and priorities of the organization. This may come in the form of allowing for decisions to be made as a group within the organization or agreeing to policies that may not have been implemented within a country had it not been a member of the organization.

Practice Questions: 10 and 11

PRACTICE QUESTIONS—RELATED ISSUE 3

1. By joining NATO and NORAD, Canada sacrificed

   A. some sovereignty in return for more security

   B. international prestige in return for economic development

   C. independent control of its armed forces in exchange for its own stockpile of nuclear weapons

   D. close economic ties with Western Europe in exchange for closer economic ties with the United States

Use the following information to answer the next question.

Proposals for Averting Nuclear Confrontation	
I	The number of nuclear weapons should be restricted to a certain level.
II	Nuclear powers should be encouraged to protect their arsenals using extreme measures.
III	The United Nations should establish a force equipped with enough military power to stop nuclear aggression.
IV	Nuclear powers and their allies should agree to not deploy nuclear weapons in the event of war.

2. Which of the given proposals formed the basis for the Strategic Arms Limitation talks?

   A. Proposal I

   B. Proposal II

   C. Proposal III

   D. Proposal IV

3. The principle of internationalism is demonstrated when nations attempt to establish

   A. colonial empires
   B. isolationist policies
   C. spheres of influence
   D. multilateral agreements

Use the following information to answer the next question.

The Republican party maintains the traditional American policy of noninterference in the political affairs of other nations. This government has definitely refused membership in the League of Nations and to assume any obligations under the covenant of the League. On this we stand. —from *Internationalism: Opposing Viewpoints*

4. Which of the following statements explains the principle upon which this declaration was **most likely** made?

   A. Containment should come before neutrality.
   B. Deterrence should come before appeasement.
   C. Sovereignty should come before collective security.
   D. International cooperation should come before national interests.

Use the following information to answer the next two questions.

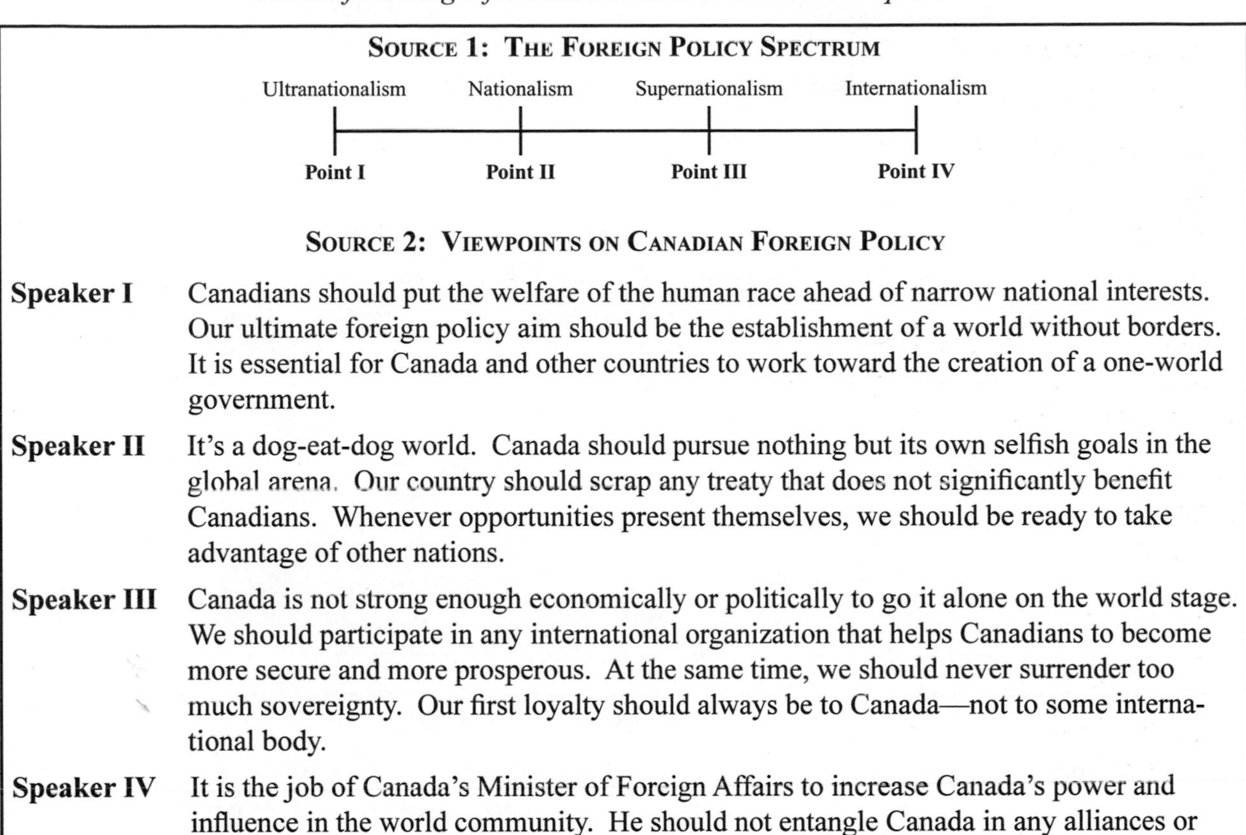

Source 1: The Foreign Policy Spectrum

Ultranationalism	Nationalism	Supernationalism	Internationalism
Point I	**Point II**	**Point III**	**Point IV**

Source 2: Viewpoints on Canadian Foreign Policy

Speaker I Canadians should put the welfare of the human race ahead of narrow national interests. Our ultimate foreign policy aim should be the establishment of a world without borders. It is essential for Canada and other countries to work toward the creation of a one-world government.

Speaker II It's a dog-eat-dog world. Canada should pursue nothing but its own selfish goals in the global arena. Our country should scrap any treaty that does not significantly benefit Canadians. Whenever opportunities present themselves, we should be ready to take advantage of other nations.

Speaker III Canada is not strong enough economically or politically to go it alone on the world stage. We should participate in any international organization that helps Canadians to become more secure and more prosperous. At the same time, we should never surrender too much sovereignty. Our first loyalty should always be to Canada—not to some international body.

Speaker IV It is the job of Canada's Minister of Foreign Affairs to increase Canada's power and influence in the world community. He should not entangle Canada in any alliances or humanitarian projects. He should cut off all foreign aid to the Third World. Canada should pursue an independent foreign policy that benefits our nation while respecting the rights of other nations.

5. Which speaker is **most** willing to surrender Canada's sovereignty in the pursuit of international cooperation?

A. Speaker I

B. Speaker II

C. Speaker III

D. Speaker IV

6. Which two speakers hold the **most similar** views on Canada's involvement in alliances?

A. Speaker I and Speaker III

B. Speaker I and Speaker IV

C. Speaker II and Speaker III

D. Speaker III and Speaker IV

7. During the Cold War, the prediction that the forces of nationalism would become less dominant in world affairs was supported by the

   A. formation of the Warsaw Pact as a response to the NATO alliance

   B. creation of defensive alliances to counter the threat of ethnic conflict

   C. decolonization of Africa and the resulting creation of many new nations

   D. formation of the Common Market in a movement toward a unified Europe

8. Which of the following organizations works **primarily** to promote international cultural diversity, especially through language?

   A. EU

   B. UN

   C. OIF

   D. Arctic Council

Use the following statement to answer the next question.

A Solution to the Debt Crisis in the Developing World

Since 1982, the developing world has been experiencing a debt crisis. Poor nations are burdened with massive debts that clearly cannot be paid and that have produced major financial, economic, and social upheavals. The creditor-nations of the North must do more to solve this debt crisis. They should ease the burden on debtor-nations by refinancing or rescheduling payments. Methods such as these must be used to ease the obligation of a debtor-nation to repay loans. Simply put, governments and banks in the developed world must take action to make repayment easier.

9. Which of the following policies would be **most favoured** by the speaker as a means of dealing with the debt crisis in the developing world?

   A. Debt relief

   B. A debt swap

   C. Debt forgiveness

   D. A debt moratorium

Use the following information to answer the next question.

10. In the given cartoon, the issue being settled with a coin toss is

A. a war

B. a debate

C. a referendum

D. a federal election

Use the following information to answer the next question.

The problem with Canada's geography is that capital cities and the vast majority of Canadians are squeezed up against Canada's southern border. This results in many problems for the country. For instance, all political power is concentrated in these southern cities, leaving northerners with no real say over their natural resources and communities. The inevitable result is the exploitation of northerners by southerners. For example, it's city-slicker politicians in Toronto, Regina, or Winnipeg who make the deals with logging companies and pulp mills that lead to the devastation of northern forests and ecosystems. These southerners are making decisions about areas they do not live in and have never even visited. Unless Canada's political map can be readjusted and the northern nine-tenths of Canada's landmass be more effectively developed and fairly treated, Canada will never realize its true potential.

11. The author seems to **most strongly** favour

A. decreased exports

B. increased urbanization

C. more development in southern regions

D. more localized management of natural resources

ANSWERS AND SOLUTIONS—PRACTICE QUESTION

1. A	**4. C**	**7. D**	**10. C**
2. A	**5. A**	**8. C**	**11. D**
3. D	**6. C**	**9. A**	

1. A

Whenever a nation joins any international organization or alliance, it must surrender some sovereignty (the ability to make its own decisions independently) because it must now collectively arrive at agreements with partner-nations. Such a surrender certainly occurred when Canada became part of the North Atlantic Treaty Organization (NATO) and the North American Aerospace Defence Command (NORAD). Both of these military alliances were Cold War-era collective security arrangements.

Membership in NATO and NORAD probably enhanced Canada's international prestige; however, they had no major impact on Canada's economy. Canada did surrender independent control of its armed forces when it joined NATO and NORAD, particularly over Canadian troops in Europe that were under joint Allied (ultimately American) command. Canada did not have its own stockpile of nuclear weapons when it joined the two alliances. NATO was primarily a military alliance, but it had characteristics of an economic agreement as well. It actually encouraged closer ties with Western European countries instead of discouraging them.

2. A

The Strategic Arms Limitation Talks (SALT) of 1969 to 1979 aimed at limiting the United States' and Soviet Union's production and deployment of nuclear weapons. Proposal I was the basis for the SALT talks.

None of the other proposals was the basis for the SALT talks.

3. D

***Internationalism* is the belief that the greatest possible cooperation between nations in trade, culture, education, government, etc., is the best way to build peace. Therefore, internationalism is demonstrated when nations enter into multilateral agreements (agreements or treaties in which three or more nation-states participate).**

Internationalism is not demonstrated when a nation conquers weaker nations, practices noninvolvement in international affairs, or dominates other nations politically or economically.

4. C

The declaration is an expression of isolationism. *Isolationism* is a belief that peace and economic advancement can best be achieved by removing one's country from alliances and commitments to other nations. Isolationism is a policy of narrow nationalism. The isolationist cares about his own country and has no real concern for the welfare of other nations. The declaration suggests that sovereignty (national independence) should take precedence over collective security (protecting weaker nations from aggression through participation in a global defensive alliance).

The declaration does not express support for containment (preventing the spread of the power or influence of an enemy country or ideology beyond the existing boundaries of its influence), deterrence (maintaining vast military power and weaponry in order to discourage war), or international cooperation. It recommends giving priority to internal affairs and national interests. It goes beyond recommending neutrality (not taking part or giving assistance in a dispute or war between other nations) by suggesting that the United States should not participate at all in the affairs of other nations.

5. A

Speaker I is an internationalist who wants to create a one-world government. This would mean the elimination of nation-states and independent national governments. Ultimately, this speaker advocates a total surrender of Canada's sovereignty.

None of the other speakers advocates a complete surrender of Canada's sovereignty.

6. C

Both Speaker II and Speaker III support Canada's participation in any international agreement or organization that benefits Canadians.

No other pair of speakers holds views on alliances that are as similar as those of speakers II and III. Speaker IV is an isolationist who wants Canada to abandon all alliances and foreign commitments. Speaker I is an internationalist who advocates alliances in the interests of all nationalities, not just of Canadians.

7. D

The formation of the Common Market and other efforts to create a more unified Europe pointed to the fact that nationalism was becoming less dominant in world affairs.

The Warsaw Pact and the NATO alliance had little or no effect on nationalism. Further, defensive alliances were not formed during the Cold War to counter the threat of ethnic conflict. During the Cold War, many nations in Africa and Asia gained their independence through the process of decolonization. The creation of new nations might make the forces of nationalism more dominant because nationalism could play a role as a competing force between these new countries and neighbouring countries trying to settle any disputes they may have over amended borders.

8. C

The OIF (*l'Organisation internationale de la Francophonie*) works to promote cultural diversity through the promotion of French as an international language.

The EU, the UN, and the Arctic Council do not have international cultural diversity as their main priority.

9. A

The speaker recommends debt relief (easing the obligations of a debtor-nation to repay loans) as a means of solving the debt crisis in the developing world. The speaker's statements support debt refinancing and the rescheduling of debt payments—both of these actions are examples of debt relief.

The speaker does not advocate a debt swap (a scheme involving the assumption of debt repayment obligations by a new nation or organization in exchange for some favour by the debtor-nation), debt forgiveness (cancelling obligations to repay debts), or a debt moratorium (the postponement of payments on loans).

10. C

The coin toss in the cartoon represents the deciding of a referendum on Quebec sovereignty. The cartoon suggests that Quebec separatists plan to keep holding referendums on separation until they finally win.

The cartoon is not referring to a war, a debate, or a federal election. *Secession* refers to "withdrawal from a political federation." It is clear that the theme of the cartoon is about Quebec referendums on Quebec separation.

11. D

The speaker appears to support more localized management of natural resources. That is, the speaker wants northern development to be controlled by northerners.

The speaker does not specifically recommend decreased exports, more development in the south, or increased urbanization in the north or south.

UNIT TEST—RELATED ISSUE 3

Use the following information to answer the next two questions.

Some day they'll come crawling back to her.

—from *A Cartoon History of United States Foreign Policy*

1. This cartoon from 1919 ridicules American political party members who supported the idea of

A. containing the spread of communism

B. appeasing aggressive European dictators

C. maintaining a balance of power through European alliances

D. employing collective security through the League of Nations

2. Advocates of the policy followed by America's "Last Republicans" and "Last Democrats" would have said that *Americanism* was just another word for

A. idealism

B. isolationism

C. ultranationalism

D. supranationalism

3. Which of the following foreign policy goals is correctly matched with the organization that Canada joined to achieve the specified goal?

	Foreign Policy Goal	Organization
A.	Promote economic cooperation in the Asia–Pacific region	G8
B.	Encourage world monetary stability and global economic development	Arctic Council
C.	Create rules for open and fair economic competition between nations	La Francophonie
D.	Maintain cooperation among former members of the British Empire	the Commonwealth

Use the following information to answer the next question.

Developments in Nuclear Disarmament

Partial Test Ban Treaty
Nuclear Non-Proliferation Treaty
Outer Space Treaty
Seabed Treaty

4. The success of these developments depended **mainly** upon the signatories' willingness to promote
   A. regional alliances
   B. international prosperity
   C. supranational cooperation
   D. technological advancement

Use the following information to answer the next question.

D-Day: landing boats, dramatic action, a known and evil foe, full power, victory. Nothing has changed more in 50 years than the way in which we tend to the global stability that was bought by massive commitment and sacrifice in the Second World War. The United Nations peacekeeping operations now scattered around the world are everything that D-Day was not: marginal, ambivalent, ragged, controversial. We must deal with the world we live in, and we live in a world where peacekeeping in its various forms is unavoidable and important to us. We have not done it well enough and as a result we face a certain crisis of internationalism.

— from *The Edmonton Journal, 1994*

5. The "crisis of internationalism" referred to in the given source can be illustrated by the decision that currently faces many nations about whether or not to
   A. involve themselves in conflicts that do not directly affect their national interest
   B. continue their membership in military alliances formed during the Cold War
   C. support serious efforts to monitor and limit environmental degradation
   D. rebuild their armed forces to protect national security

6. Originally, the European Common Market was formed to

A. establish competitive trade rivalries

B. halt Communist expansion in the area

C. encourage greater economic prosperity

D. compete with the North American Free Trade Agreement

Use the following information to answer the next two questions.

Some Articles from the Treaties of Rome
– A common agricultural policy shall be established among Member States.
– A common transportation policy shall be created for Member States.
– A common tariff and trade policy among Member States shall be pursued.
– Tariff and trade restrictions among Member States shall be abolished.
– People, capital, and services shall move freely between Member States.

7. These articles were to serve as the basis for the formation of the

A. Allied Control Council in 1946

B. North Atlantic Treaty Organization in 1949

C. Council for Mutual Economic Assistance in 1949

D. European Economic Community in 1957

8. By accepting and acting upon the given articles, the member-governments demonstrated their commitment to the principle of

A. national sovereignty

B. national security

C. ultranationalism

D. internationalism

9. The participation of Canadian soldiers in the supervision of the ceasefire that ended the 1980–88 Iraq–Iran War **best** illustrates Canada's ongoing commitment to the principle of

A. national security

B. global prosperity

C. collective security

D. international equality

10. Many Canadians believe that memberships in NATO and NORAD are in Canada's national interest because they provide Canadians with
   A. more security
   B. greater prosperity
   C. enhanced sovereignty
   D. improved transportation and communication links

11. The attempt to improve the welfare of a nation through health, education, and housing programs is called
   A. multilateral aid
   B. social development
   C. structural adjustment
   D. economic development

Use the following information to answer the next two questions.

Source I – Definitions of Foreign Policy Approaches

Isolationism	A policy that advocates nonparticipation in alliances or in the affairs of other states
Internationalism	Support for maximum cooperation between nations, possibly to the extent of advocating the creation of a world without national borders
Humanitarianism	Support for the general welfare of the human race and for the relief of the pain and suffering of all human beings, regardless of their nationality
Supranationalism	The belief that nations should cooperate for their mutual benefit by creating international organizations, laws, and accords

Source II – Statement

The world community must move promptly toward comprehensive treaties to protect the air, soil, and water. A framework for the effort exists within the United Nations, which has already taken some important initiatives. Every country should realize that such treaties are in its national interest. Environmental protection agreements will not negatively impact on national sovereignty, and these agreements certainly will not lead to a one-world government. Global government that allows for the maintenance of sovereignty is something that should be considered in order to achieve cooperation on a global scale.

12. Which of the given foreign policy approaches seems to be **most favoured** by the speaker of the statement in Source II?
   A. Isolationism
   B. Internationalism
   C. Humanitarianism
   D. Supranationalism

13. Which of the given foreign policy approaches would **most likely** be supported by the international organization Amnesty International?

A. Isolationism

B. Internationalism

C. Humanitarianism

D. Supranationalism

14. Canada's signing of which of the following statutes demonstrates its commitment to internationalism?

A. The Bill of Rights

B. The Charter of Rights and Freedoms

C. The Individual Rights Protection Act

D. The Universal Declaration of Human Rights

15. A country seeking economic stability would **most likely** seek membership in which of the following organizations?

A. G8

B. NATO

C. United Nations

D. La Francophonie

Use the following information to answer the next question.

> Our country must be careful not to get too chummy with other countries and should carefully decide which international organizations we should belong to. Our first and foremost concern must be for the well-being of our government and the citizens of the country. Pride in our country and a desire to do what's best for it must stay at the forefronts of our politicians' and citizens' minds. We can't allow for the decisions being made in and about our country to be manipulated or controlled by others.

16. With which of the following issues is the speaker in the source **most** concerned?

A. Maintaining sovereignty

B. Achieving economic stability

C. Maintaining defensive alliances

D. Promoting humanitarian policies

Use the following information to answer the next three questions.

Organization I	Provide economic assistance to struggling economies
Organization II	Promote economic cooperation and trade across Europe
Organization III	Provide a forum for discussion on international economic issues
Organization IV	Promote international cooperation on issues facing the Arctic Circle

17. Which of the given organizations represents the IMF?

A. Organization I

B. Organization II

C. Organization III

D. Organization IV

18. Members of which of the given organizations use a common currency to further their goals?

A. Organization I

B. Organization II

C. Organization III

D. Organization IV

19. Climate change and sustainable development are two of the main issues addressed by the mandates of which of the given organizations?

A. Organization I

B. Organization II

C. Organization III

D. Organization IV

Use the following information to answer the next question.

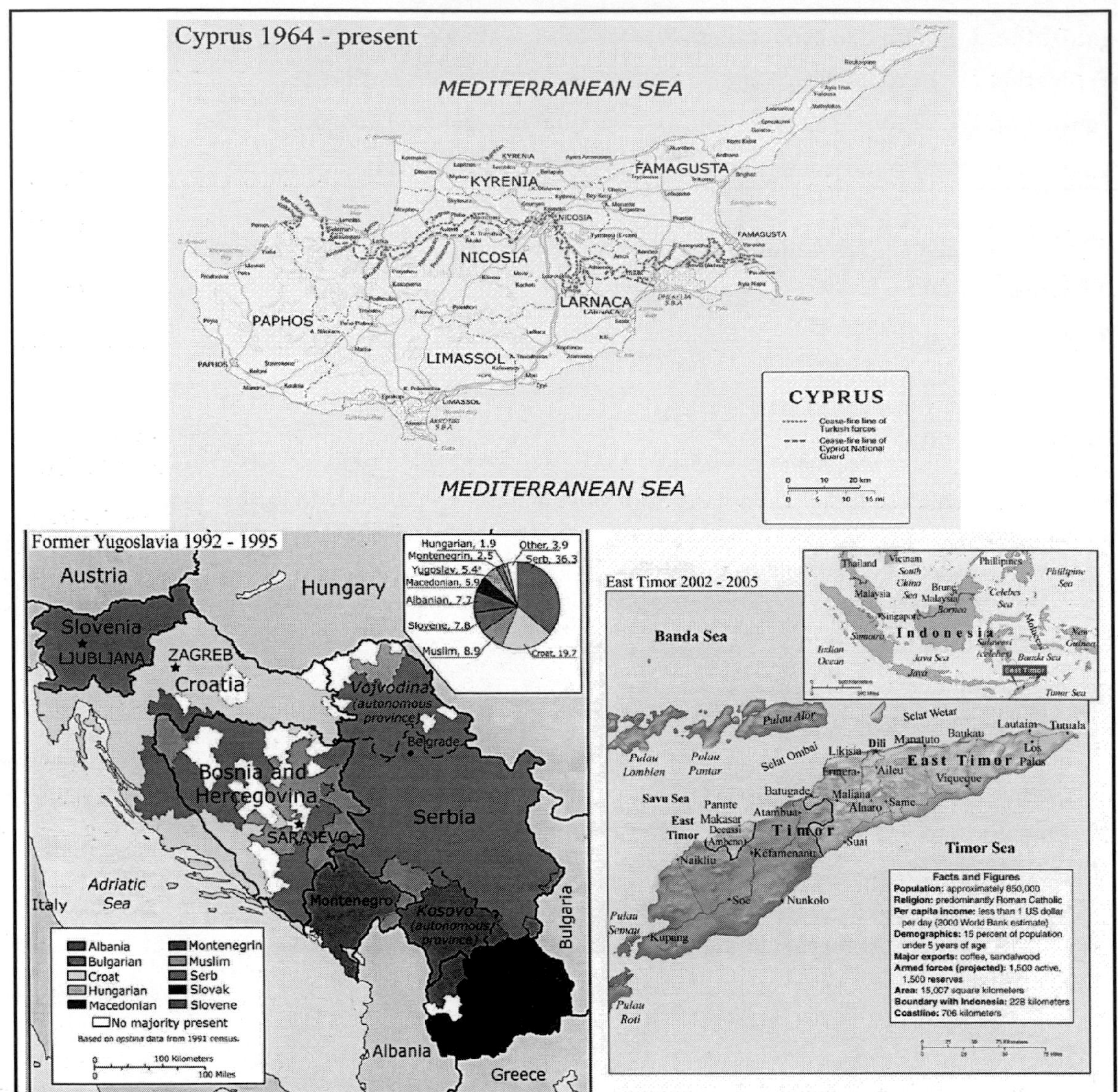

20. One thing that each of the given locations has in common is that each is or has been

A. a developed nation

B. a Communist country

C. expelled from the United Nations

D. the site of a multilateral peacekeeping operation

ANSWERS AND SOLUTIONS—UNIT TEST

1. D	**5. A**	**9. C**	**13. C**	**17. A**
2. B	**6. C**	**10. A**	**14. D**	**18. B**
3. D	**7. D**	**11. B**	**15. A**	**19. D**
4. C	**8. D**	**12. B**	**16. A**	**20. D**

1. **D**

The given cartoon shows the traditional America-first philosophy being abandoned by American politicians who have turned their attentions away from domestic politics and toward international affairs. This cartoon ridicules American politicians like Woodrow Wilson who placed great hope in the philosophy of internationalism (a concern for the general welfare of humanity), the League of Nations, and the concept of collective security (the principle that member-states of the League of Nations would act together to stop aggression).

The cartoon does not ridicule communism, appeasement, or a balance of power system.

2. **B**

In the cartoon, *Americanism* refers to an "America-first" philosophy, which is a synonym for *isolationism.*

In the cartoon, the term *Americanism* does not refer to idealism (the pursuit of idealistic goals), ultranationalism (the willingness to go to extreme lengths to increase the power and prosperity of one's nation-state), or supranationalism (support for the creation of international organizations and international laws).

3. **D**

The Commonwealth maintains cooperation between Britain and its former colonies.

APEC is the organization for Asia–Pacific economic cooperation; the G8 is a meeting of eight of the world's industrialized, democratic countries. The IMF encourages world monetary stability and global economic development; the Arctic Council addresses issues facing Arctic nations and their citizens. The WTO creates rules for open and fair economic competition; *La Francophonie* is a group of countries with French-speaking citizens and French culture that works to promote the French language and culture worldwide.

4. **C**

Supranationalism is the belief that nations should set aside national differences and cooperate for their mutual benefit. All of these arms control agreements are examples of supranational cooperation. In the 1963 Partial Test Ban Treaty, the United States, Britain, and the Soviet Union agreed not to test nuclear weapons in the atmosphere, in outer space, or underwater. The treaty was an attempt to stop an alarming rise in worldwide radioactive pollution levels. In the 1968 Non-Proliferation Treaty, these nuclear powers committed themselves to preventing the spread of nuclear weapons technology to new countries. In the 1967 Outer Space Treaty and the 1971 Seabed Treaty, nuclear powers pledged to not deploy nuclear weapons in outer space or on the ocean floor.

Arms control agreements do not depend on signatories' willingness to promote regional alliances, international prosperity, or technological advancement.

5. A

Fulfilling the goal of maintaining peace in the modern world faces a serious problem—many conflicts occur in areas of the world that are often considered unimportant to nations that have the capability of enforcing world order. As a result, many conflicts are allowed to continue for months or even years without resolution.

As a result of the instability in the world, alliances like NATO have maintained their membership or increased it by adding former members of the Warsaw Pact, such as Poland. There is nothing in the given source that is concerned with the environment. Few of the world's nations need to rebuild their armed forces—most nations have military forces that exceed their needs in a time of so-called peace.

6. C

The Common Market (European Economic Community or EEC) was established in the 1950s to stimulate economic prosperity through encouragement of trade, reduction of trade barriers, and freer movement of labour and capital between member countries.

The goal of the Common Market was to promote economic cooperation between Western European states. It was not designed to encourage stiffer economic competition. The halting of Communist expansion was more a concern of the Marshall Plan and the NATO alliance. The Marshall Plan and NATO both preceded the European Common Market, and the EEC lacked the anti-communist political agenda of the Marshall Plan and NATO. The EEC was in place by 1957, and NAFTA did not come into effect until 1994.

7. D

The Treaties of Rome (March 25, 1957) created the European Economic Community (European Common Market), the forerunner of today's European Union.

The given articles are not related to the formation of the Allied Control Council, NATO, or the Council for Mutual Economic Assistance.

8. D

Internationalism is the belief in the importance of cooperation among countries in order to promote the common good for all countries, both socially and economically. By being part of the European Union (the successor to the Treaty of Rome), members were demonstrating their commitment to internationalism.

Membership in the European Common Market (EEC) necessitated the surrender of some national sovereignty. When a nation joins together with other nations to create common economic policies, it will no longer have complete control over its own economy. The European Economic Community brought about economic integration; it did not enhance the national security of western European nations. Ultranationalism (extreme or excessive nationalism) is not the same thing as supranationalism (support for the creation of international laws, agreements, and organizations by national governments).

9. C

The United Nation's supervision of the Iran–Iraq ceasefire is a classic example of international peacekeeping efforts by the United Nations through military force. Involvement in any peacekeeping mission demonstrates a commitment to the principle of collective security. Collective security is a policy or principle of international relations through which countries collectively guarantee the security of individual countries in order to preserve world peace.

The efforts of Canada's UN peacekeepers in the Middle East do not demonstrate Canada's commitment to global prosperity, its own national security, or international equality. The Canadian peacekeepers were simply trying to prevent hostilities from breaking out again between Iraq and Iran.

10. A

The North Atlantic Treaty Organization (NATO) and the North American Aerospace Defense Command (NORAD) are two of Canada's military defensive alliances. Canada surrenders some sovereignty by belonging to these two alliances, but it gains more security in return.

NATO and NORAD memberships are not intended to enhance Canada's economic prosperity, transportation links, or communications links. When Canada joins any international or supranational organization, it surrenders some sovereignty (independent control of its own affairs), since it now must make decisions collectively with its partner-nation(s).

11. B

Social development is improvement in the welfare of the people of a society, including programs contributing to better health and education, decent housing, and access to basic services.

Multilateral aid is aid channelled by two or more donor countries through international organizations to carry out projects in developing countries. The term *structural adjustment* refers to measures undertaken by a government over a long time to change the fundamental structure of the country's economy in order to correct severe economic problems and re-establish economic growth. Economic development differs from social development by focusing more on the production of goods and services through increased industry and trade; economic development strives for increased economic production rather than for the improvement of human beings—the latter is the chief goal of social development.

12. B

The speaker shows support for internationalism by suggesting consideration of a global government that still allows for sovereignty.

Although supranationalism is something that may be supported by the speaker, a global government calls for more integrated involvement of countries than supranationalism suggests. The speaker does not show support for isolationism or humanitarianism.

13. C

Amnesty International (AI) promotes human rights for people around the world and would be most supportive of humanitarian foreign policies.

None of the other approaches would be more supported by AI than humanitarianism.

14. D

By signing the Universal Declaration of Human Rights, Canada joined other countries in publicly asserting its belief that everyone is entitled to basic human rights and in pledging to adhere to international standards.

The 1960 Bill of Rights, the Individual Rights Protection Act, and the 1982 Charter of Rights and Freedoms were all events that had an effect on Canada domestically but did not reflect Canada's commitment to internationalism.

15. A

The G8 (Group of Eight) is an international organization of eight of the wealthiest countries in the world who meet to discuss issues of international importance, in particular those associated with economics.

NATO (North Atlantic Treaty Organization) is primarily a defence alliance. Neither membership in the United Nations nor *La Francophonie* would fulfill the primary goal of economic stability, as several nations that are part of these organizations are considered to be developing nations that struggle with economic stability.

16. A

The speaker expresses concern that becoming too involved in international organizations may lead to a loss of sovereignty or some sacrifice of nationalism within his or her country.

Neither economic stability, the maintenance of defensive alliances, nor the promotion of humanitarian policies are addressed by the speaker.

17. A

The IMF (International Monetary Fund) is an international organization that works to promote global economic stability and provides assistance to struggling economies in order to reduce debt and poverty.

Organization II represents the European Union. Organization III represents the Group of Eight. Organization IV represents the Arctic Council.

18. B

Organization II represents the European Union (EU). Several members of the EU have adopted a common currency (the euro) to facilitate their economic goals.

The International Monetary Fund (Organization I), the Group of Eight (Organization II), and the Arctic Council (Organization IV) have not adopted a common currency.

19. D

Organization IV represents the Arctic Council, which is an international organization of nations with interest in the Arctic. Two main concerns for the Arctic region are climate change and sustainable development.

The International Monetary Fund (Organization I), the European Union (Organization II), and the Group of Eight (Organization III) do not have these two concerns as their main goals.

20. D

Each of the locations listed in the source was the site of a multilateral peacekeeping operation conducted by the United Nations during the dates provided.

None of the countries are or have been developed nations, communist countries, or expelled from the United Nations.

Related Issue 4

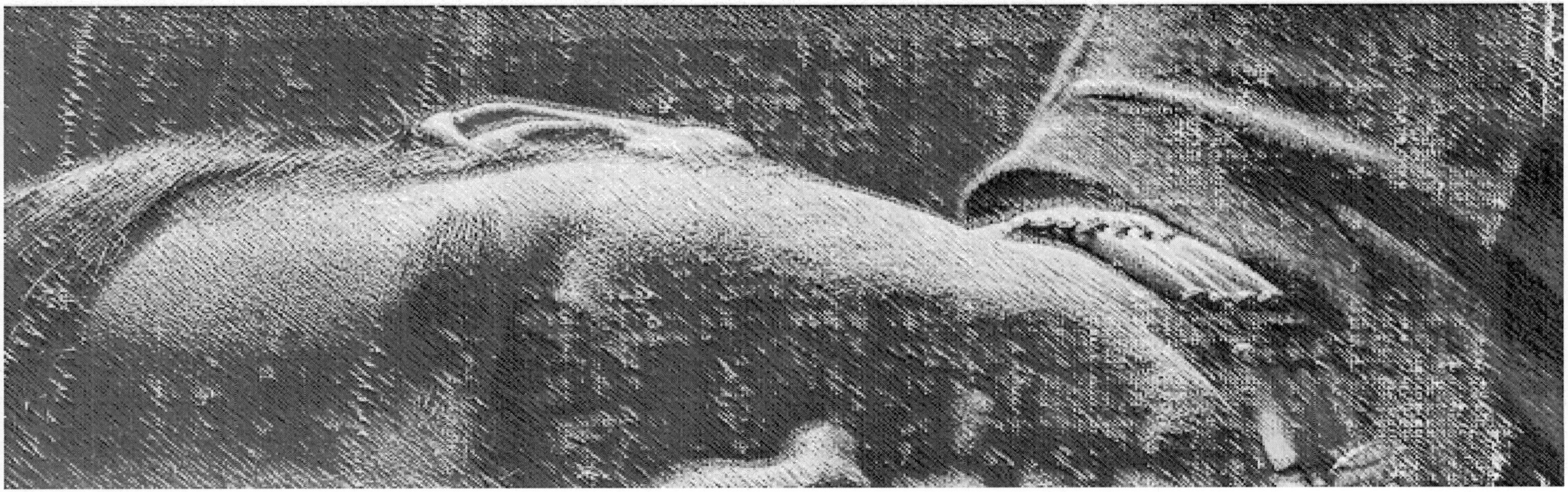

RELATED ISSUE 4

Table of Correlations

Specific Outcome	Practice Questions	Unit Test Questions	Practice Test 1	Practice Test 2
Students will assess strategies for negotiating the complexities of nationalism within the Canadian context.				
4.4 explore multiple perspectives on national identity in Canada	1, 2		28	
4.5 analyze methods used by individuals, groups and governments in Canada to promote a national identity (symbolism, mythology, institutions, government programs and initiatives)	3	8, 9	40, 41	44
4.6 examine historical perspectives of Canada as a nation (Louis Lafontaine and Robert Baldwin, the Fathers of Confederation, First Nations treaties and the Indian Act, Métis and Inuit self-governance, Louis Riel, Sir Clifford Sifton, Henri Bourassa, French-Canadian nationalism, Pierre Trudeau, National Indian Brotherhood)	4, 5	1, 2, 3, 12, 13, 14, 16, 19	42, 43, 44	15, 15, 45, 46
4.7 evaluate the challenges and opportunities associated with the promotion of Canadian national unity (Québec sovereignty, federal–provincial–territorial relations, Aboriginal self-determination and land claims, bilingualism, multiculturalism)	6, 7	4, 10, 11	26, 27	11, 12, 13
4.8 evaluate various perspectives of future visions of Canada (pluralism, multination model, separatism, Aboriginal self-determination, global leadership, North American integration)	8, 9	5, 6, 7, 15, 17, 18	6	47, 48, 49

RELATED ISSUE 4

To What Extent Should Individuals and Groups in Canada Embrace a National Identity?

4.4 explore multiple perspectives on national identity in Canada

National Identity in Canada

Within Canada, there are many different perspectives on Canadian national identity. Many people in Canada identify themselves not only as Canadian but also as part of another ethnic, cultural, or religious group. Different regions of Canada have different perspectives on what it is to be Canadian. Part of Canada's national identity is that Canada is a **pluralistic society**, which means that there are people of many different cultural and ethnic groups living within the country.

Living in a pluralistic or multicultural society can mean that some people do not identify themselves as being fully Canadian. For example, across Canada, there are people who regard themselves as being Italian-Canadian, African-Canadian, or Chinese-Canadian, among many others. These people often have ancestry in another country, and they want to maintain the culture and traditions associated with their ancestral country while enjoying Canadian citizenship and embracing Canadian traditions and ways of life. People who are members of a religious group sometimes identify primarily with their religious group and secondarily with their country.

Some people in Canada identify themselves not only with Canada but with their region. In Quebec, many Francophones see themselves as Quebecers before Canadians. Some Quebecers believe Quebec should be considered a separate nation within Canada because of its unique culture and language. Maritimers and Westerners may also feel a stronger sense of identity with other people in their region than with Canadians in general.

Canada's Aboriginal people often feel a sense of nationhood among themselves. Some Aboriginal people do not view themselves as Canadians but as members of a separate nation within Canada.

Practice Questions: 1 and 2

4.5 analyze methods used by individuals, groups and governments in Canada to promote a national identity (symbolism, mythology, institutions, government programs and initiatives)

Methods to Promote National Identity

Individuals and groups within Canada use various methods to promote a national identity. Symbolism is used to help people in Canada feel a sense of belonging and sameness with other Canadians. For example, the Maple Leaf is a symbol that is internationally recognized as Canadian, and many Canadians feel it is a way of defining who they are. Both at home and abroad, many Canadians feel a sense of pride and nationhood when they see a Maple Leaf or wear one on their clothing. It helps to identify them as Canadian, and it is something that only Canadians share.

Mythology is another way of promoting national identity, since it often involves stories of grandeur or bravery that tell the history of a country or nation. These stories are often passed between generations as a way to teach a person's historical connection with the country or nation.

Institutions can also promote a national identity. Some institutions influence the way the international community views a country or are closely associated with the history of a country. An institution that works to promote Canadian identity is the Canadian Broadcasting Corporation (CBC). The CBC is a media institution that provides information to Canadians about important issues through the Internet, radio, and television. Information from the CBC is available in both French and English, and the CBC works to promote the achievements of Canadians in a broad spectrum of activities. For Canadians, it is a source of news about the government as well as about domestic and foreign affairs. Another example of a Canadian institution that promotes national identity is the Royal Canadian Mounted Police (RCMP). The RCMP evolved from the North West Mounted Police and so, has been a part of Canada since shortly after Confederation. The red uniform of the Mounties is recognized worldwide as being Canadian. Canada is also recognized for its peacekeeping forces. These peacekeepers have helped Canada gain an international reputation as a peace-loving nation, which has led to Canadian national pride.

Government programs and initiatives also play a role in promoting a national identity. Government organizations such as the Canadian Radio-television and Telecommunications Commission (CRTC), the National Film Board, and Telefilm Canada help to promote and fund Canadian media. Through Canadian media, Canadians are exposed to Canadian talent, issues, and culture, which better enables them to develop a sense of nationhood. In addition, the Department of Canadian Heritage works to strengthen connections among Canadians through the promotion of Canadian culture and traditions. This department provides funding for some local heritage festivals that celebrate Canada's multiculturalism while bringing people of different backgrounds together. It also promotes art and sport in Canada and works to promote national identity among Canada's youth by sponsoring initiatives such as the "Celebrate Canada!" poster challenge and exchange programs that allow youth in Canada to experience life through the eyes of Canadians in different regions of the country.

Related Question: 3

4.6 *examine historical perspectives of Canada as a nation (Louis Lafontaine and Robert Baldwin, the Fathers of Confederation, First Nations treaties and the Indian Act, Métis and Inuit self-governance, Louis Riel, Sir Clifford Sifton, Henri Bourassa, French-Canadian nationalism, Pierre Trudeau, National Indian Brotherhood)*

Canada as a Nation in History

Historical events have an effect on the development of a nation's identity, and the influence of some individuals and groups on that development of identity is more significant that that of others. Consider the following individuals and groups and the effect they have each had on Canadian identity.

Louis-Hippolyte Lafontaine, who was from Lower Canada, became the Prime Minister of the United Province of Canada in 1842 when Upper and Lower Canada were joined into one legislative assembly. Lafontaine worked hard to promote and maintain the French language without the use of violence, and he did not support the violent uprising that took place between the French and English. Lafontaine wanted a united Canada in which both French and English could exist together. Lafontaine worked closely with Robert Baldwin, who was from Upper Canada, to establish responsible government in Canada, which still exists today as one of the cornerstones of Canadian democracy. Together Lafontaine and Baldwin led a Reform government and introduced many reforms, including the adoption of responsible government and changes to the judicial system in Canada. Like Lafontaine, Baldwin viewed Canada as a country in which French and English were equal.

The men who became known as the **Fathers of Confederation** were the leaders of the colonies that participated in the conferences that led to the creation of the British North America Act, which made Canada a country in 1867. After the union of Upper and Lower Canada in 1841, there was unrest as both French and English citizens struggled to reconcile their differences. The Fathers of Confederation believed that constitutional reform was necessary to unite Canada, and they met together at the conferences that eventually led to Confederation. Perhaps the most famous of this group of men is Sir John A. Macdonald, who became the first prime minister of Canada. He dreamed of uniting the country, not only with ideas but with something tangible—the Canadian Pacific Railway—which he believed would help Canada develop as a country. Macdonald helped to convince more provinces to join Confederation and paved the way for others to join the new country soon after Confederation.

Louis Riel lived in Manitoba, where he was a leader of the Métis people during the mid-1800s. He was concerned about the Canadian government's intentions to expand into the Western territories without regard for the Métis way of life. After seizing Ft. Garry and becoming head of a provisional government in 1869, Riel drafted a Metis Bill of Rights and outlined the conditions under which Manitoba should become a province. During this uprising, a certain Thomas Scott who strongly opposed Riel and the Metis, was executed. In 1875, Riel was exiled from Canada for a period of five years for his earlier role in Scott's death. Historians continue to debate whether Riel was a friend or foe of Canadian nationalism and the building of the nation.

Sir Clifford Sifton is best known for his promotion of immigration in the western part of Canada. He was concerned about issues facing the people of the Prairies and worked hard to defend these people. Sifton believed it was important to populate the West, and he pioneered for aggressive immigration policies that opened the door for thousands of European immigrants to come to Western Canada.

Henri Bourassa was very active in Canadian politics and advocated strongly that Canada should be Anglo-French. He believed that French citizens should not be assimilated into English culture, and that the preservation of French culture and language was imperative if Francophone participation in Confederation was to continue. Although he was not supportive of a separate French state, Bourassa insisted that the preservation of French culture was paramount to the unity of Canada. He also resented the British influence in Canadian government. Bourassa vehemently opposed Canadian involvement in both the Second Boer War and the First World War because the cabinet did not consult Parliament. Bourassa believed the decision to go to war should have been solely Canada's, not Britain's, and he was concerned that it set a precedent for Canada to automatically become involved in Britain's conflicts.

Pierre Elliot Trudeau was the prime minister of Canada from 1968 to 1979 and again from 1980 to 1984. A member of the Liberal party, he is often considered to be one of Canada's most influential politicians. Prior to becoming prime minister, as minister of justice, he introduced several controversial laws regarding divorce, abortion, and gay rights. During the time that Trudeau was prime minister of Canada, he was renown for his strong advocacy of a united Canada and his opposition to a separate Quebec. While Trudeau was prime minister, the separatist movement was very strong in Quebec. In October 1970, a terrorist organization called the Front de libération du Québec (FLQ) staged a violent protest during which they kidnapped two government officials, James Cross (later released by the FLQ) and Pierre Laporte (later murdered by the FLQ). Trudeau took a hard stand against the FLQ, refusing to back down and invoking the controversial War Measures Act, which took away many civil liberties and gave the government extensive controls. Trudeau believed that both French and English must be part of Canada, and he tried to improve relations between the Quebec and Canadian governments by introducing the Official Languages Act in 1969. Unfortunately, this caused tension in other parts of the country. Western Canadians believed him to be more concerned about the issues of French Canadians than those of the West, and feelings of Western alienation developed. As a result of his commitment to embracing Canada's multiculturalism, Trudeau introduced the official Multiculturalism Policy in 1971. This policy promoted the pluralism of Canada and tolerance for different cultures, ethnicities, and religions within Canada's structure of individual rights.

Trudeau further demonstrated his commitment to Canadian confederacy in 1982 when he patriated the Constitution from Great Britain, making Canada a completely sovereign nation. In addition, the Charter of Rights and Freedoms was added to the constitution, reinforcing his belief in the importance of individual freedoms. Trudeau was concerned about American influence in Canada and was often openly critical of American economic and foreign policies. This led to tension within Canada, as many people believed that it was Trudeau's fault that American economic policies were sometimes detrimental to the Canadian economy. Since his death in 2000, Trudeau remains a controversial person in Canadian history. Some people view him as the ultimate federalist who fought his entire political career for unity and pride in Canada, while others believe he created deep divisions between groups such as French and English citizens and West and Central Canada.

Canadian nationalism has also been shaped by groups within Canada. **French Canadian nationalism** is a feeling of nationhood among Francophones in Canada who wish to preserve the French language and culture in Canada. The feeling has roots in the beliefs of some Francophones that Canada and its government do not understand the complexities of the French Canadian culture. They identify themselves as a distinct group within Canada, and some even desire that Quebec become a separate nation within Canada.

As Canada became more populated by European immigrants, issues between First Nations people and the Canadian government began to arise. Out of these came many **First Nations treaties**: agreements made both before and after Confederation between the Canadian government and First Nations people. Under these treaties, First Nations people agreed to give up much of their land and move to reserves; in exchange, the government promised them money, goods, and various other terms. Over time, the terms of these treaties have become major issues in Canada as First Nations people and the government clash over the administration of these treaties. First Nations people often feel that the government did not fulfill their obligations under the treaties and that certain rights and privileges given to the First Nations people are not being respected by the government. The challenge that exists today is to try to respect the treaties in current society and culture, which is vastly different from when the treaties were made.

Métis and Inuit people have also struggled with the government as a result of attempts made in the past to assimilate them into Canadian society. Métis and Inuit self-governance is a way for these groups to view themselves as a nation within Canada, preserving the unique cultures and traditions held by each.

Early in Canada's history, the federal government introduced the Indian Act (1876), under which the government was given the right to manage the affairs and lands of First Nations people. It was also an attempt to assimilate First Nations people into Canadian culture, as many parts of the act were racist and detrimental to the preservation of First Nations culture. The act defined an "Indian" and the rights that accompanied "treaty status" and made it difficult for First Nations people to maintain their status and the rights associated with that status. Although there have been many amendments made to the Indian Act, some people still consider it a racist piece of legislation.

The **National Indian Brotherhood** (NIB) was an organization formed in 1968 to represent Status and Treaty Aboriginal groups in Canada. The NIB worked to promote the issues and concerns of its members and also helped to bring the issue of Aboriginal self-government to the forefront of Canadian politics. The NIB believed that many of the laws in Canada were racist and detrimental to the preservation of First Nations culture in Canada. The organization is most noted for its vocal opposition of the White Paper of 1969, in which the Minister of Indian Affairs of the day, Jean Chrétien, proposed the abolition of the Indian Act and the assimilation of First Nations people into mainstream Canadian society and culture. Largely as a result of the lobbying efforts of the NIB, the White Paper was defeated. In 1982, the NIB undertook a major revision of its structure and changed its name to the Assembly of First Nations, which lobbies on behalf of First Nations peoples today.

Practice Questions: 4 and 5

4.7 evaluate the challenges and opportunities associated with the promotion of Canadian national unity (Quebec sovereignty, federal–provincial–territorial relations, Aboriginal self-determination and land claims, bilingualism, multiculturalism)

The Promotion of Canadian National Unity

Within Canada, there are both challenges and opportunities relating to the promotion of Canadian unity. As a relatively young country with a pluralistic society, balancing the needs of various cultural groups with a common Canadian identity can be a challenge. The issue of Quebec sovereignty has caused division among Canadians. Feelings of being misunderstood and concern for the loss of a language and culture have driven the Quebec sovereignty movement to demand attention and action from the Canadian government. As a result, other regions in Canada have felt the federal government is too worried about the concerns of French Canadians and that Quebec is given special treatment and concessions. Many people, both French and English, believe that French language and culture is as important to Canada's identity and history as English language and culture. Canadian unity has been threatened because of the Quebec sovereignty movement on several occasions, in particular during the October Crisis of 1970. Two major attempts to reconcile calls for Quebec sovereignty with Canadian unity took place under former prime minister Brian Mulroney, who attempted to amend the Constitution to satisfy the concerns of French Canada through the Meech Lake and Charlottetown accords. Both attempts were unsuccessful, but the sovereignty movement has been less vocal since the mid-1990s.

Federal–provincial–territorial relations are also an issue in Canadian unity. Provinces and territories often claim that the federal government does not know what is best for their respective regions and call for more autonomy and decision-making power. However, many Canadians believe that central to Canada's identity is the fact that all Canadians should have the same opportunities and access to services, regardless of where they live. In order to achieve this equality, the federal government must have some control over the laws and policies that affect all Canadians. Western alienation has presented challenges to Canadian unity, as some westerners feel the federal government is unconcerned with the issues facing the western provinces. Westerners have viewed some federal government policies as detrimental to the western provinces. Many Westerners are also opposed to the system of proportional representation used by the federal government because it results in many more federal government seats being held by representatives of Quebec and Ontario than by representatives of other parts of Canada. In addition, issues such as resource sharing and transfer payments have caused tension between the provinces and the federal government.

Aboriginal self-determination presents other challenges to national unity as the government must reconcile past agreements and wrongdoings with the First Nations, Métis, and Inuit communities within the context of the 21st century. Furthermore, Aboriginal self-determination means different things to each of the groups represented by the term *Aboriginal*—First Nations, Inuit, and Métis. In general, self-determination would allow each group to govern itself with fewer ties to the federal and provincial governments in certain areas, primarily those to do with everyday life. These include, but are not limited to, health, education, social services, policing, and alternative judiciary processes. Individual communities would be able to take directions based on what they believe to be in the best interest of that community. The governments and laws set up under these forms of self-determination would have to be reconcilable to the Canadian Constitution and the Criminal Code.

Another issue related to Canadian unity and the Aboriginal population is related to land claims. Aboriginal groups are working with the federal government to come to agreements regarding two types of land claims that stem primarily from the treaties that were signed by Aboriginal groups and the Canadian/British governments from the 1700s to the early 1900s. One type of claim is "specific" and involves land over which the government did not fulfill its obligations as laid out by various agreements or treaties. Often, these types of claims are resolved through monetary settlements or correction of the issue. The second type of claim is "comprehensive" and involves the use of land by Aboriginal people (e.g., ownership of land, hunting and fishing rights). Land claims have caused some disharmony in Canada because some people feel that the rights held by Aboriginal people are unfair or detrimental to non-Aboriginal people. Others feel that reconciling some of these issues and claims could have a very positive impact on the feeling of unity between Aboriginal people and the federal government. The largest land claim settlement in Canadian history took place between the Canadian government and the Inuit with the settlement of the Nunavut Land Claims Agreement in 1993. This agreement gave the Inuit control over large areas of the eastern region of the Northwest Territories, comprehensive mineral rights, and payments from the federal government totalling $1 billion over 14 years. The Inuit are also able to participate in discussions concerning resource and land use. In 1999, Canada's third territory, Nunavut, was officially established. Approximately 85% of the population of Nunavut is comprised of Inuit people. The Inuit in Nunavut now have their own government that regulates areas such as health, education, and social services, among others. The Métis are the third group of Aboriginal people in Canada seeking self-determination. In 1990, the Métis Settlement Act was passed in Alberta; it gave ownership of eight different areas in Alberta to the Métis. The Alberta settlements are the only ones of their kind in Canada, although there are Métis living in other parts of the country who are still working toward self-determination.

Bilingualism in Canada also affects Canadian unity since the country recognizes both French and English as official languages. English is by far the dominant language in Canada, and most new immigrants to Canada choose to learn English over French. Ensuring that French remains an integral part of Canada's identity is a challenge for the federal government. The fact that Canada is a multicultural society presents its own challenges and opportunities. Canada is widely viewed as a tolerant, multicultural nation in which people are encouraged to retain their cultural, religious, or linguistic roots. As a result, there are people of many different backgrounds living in Canada, and this diversity is often celebrated across the country. However, this very acceptance of diversity can pose a challenge because people may struggle to define what it means to be Canadian. Characteristics that define a culture, such as religion, language, artistic traditions, and traditional attire, are not common to Canadians, as they are in other countries. Sometimes, it is difficult to balance the belief in the rights of people to maintain their culture and religion with the maintenance of Canadian traditions or laws. Examples of how difficult this balance is to achieve can be seen in recent issues, such as whether or not to allow Sikh members of the RCMP to wear turbans, whether or not to allow female Muslim soccer players to wear hijabs, and to what extent religion (in particular Christianity) should be present in public schools. Reconciling these types of issues within the context of Canadian law and tradition can sometimes be difficult.

Practice Questions: 6 and 7

4.8 evaluate various perspectives of future visions of Canada (pluralism, multination model, separatism, Aboriginal self-determination, global leadership, North American integration)

FUTURE VISIONS OF CANADA

The various future visions of Canada include the **multination model**. In this model, government systems are organized to allow a minority group to have a form of self-government and form a majority in a specific area within the confines of a larger nation. For example, Quebec has a French majority with its own provincial government, even though French-speaking people make up a minority in Canada as a whole. Further to this, some people see separatism as a viable future model for Canada. In this model, Quebec would form a sovereign nation within Canada; it would have its own system of governance and laws but retain some ties to Canada in the areas such as national defence and currency. Separatism has been an issue in Canada for a long time, as French Canadians have often felt that their unique issues and concerns have not been appropriately acknowledged and dealt with by the Canadian government.

Aboriginal self-determination is a vision that many Aboriginal groups hope to see realized in Canada. If realized, Aboriginal groups would have the power to form a type of self-government that would give them control over issues affecting the everyday lives of Aboriginals. Many Aboriginal people believe that this control would not only allow them to protect and promote their culture, but would also help them deal with many of the social issues that plague the Aboriginal community.

Somewhat contrary to these visions for Canada is pluralism. This is the idea that there are many different religious, ethnic, and cultural groups in Canada and that finding a way for each of them to have an impact on the governance of Canada would be most beneficial. Others see a future for Canada as a global leader in many areas. Human rights, environmental protection, and economic sustainability are areas in which some people believe Canada should be able to promote development and change. As globalization increases and countries become more and more dependant on each other, many people believe Canada should and will have a reputation as a leader in these and other areas.

North American integration is another vision related to Canada's future. Since the introduction of NAFTA in 1994, Canada, the United States, and Mexico have begun to integrate their economies. However, these countries have the opportunity to take this integration further in other areas, such as immigration, law development and enforcement, and policies on environmental issues. Whether or not this level of integration should occur is debated. Many people are concerned that the benefits of integration would be outweighed by the negative results of the loss of sovereignty that would be required to achieve this type of integration. Other people contend that in order to remain competitive with other parts of the world that are working toward integration, North American integration is essential.

Practice Questions: 8 and 9

PRACTICE QUESTIONS—RELATED ISSUE 4

1. As a result of their shared experience in the First World War, Canadians stopped thinking of themselves as

   A. colonials

   B. nationalists

   C. North Americans

   D. constitutional monarchists

Use the following information to answer the next question.

2. The differing motivations of the soldiers in 1914 and 1939 are **most likely** a result of

   A. increased faith in the League of Nations

   B. the development of a Canadian national consciousness

   C. decreasing support for the terms of the Treaty of Versailles

   D. diminished immigration levels from Britain during the interwar era

3. The term *sovereignty* refers to

   A. a nation's royal family

   B. a country in which people are very nationalistic

   C. a nation's power to govern itself and make its own decisions

   D. the territory, territorial waters, and national air space of a country

4. Louis Riel was instrumental in the establishment of which Canadian province?

   A. British Columbia

   B. Saskatchewan

   C. Manitoba

   D. Alberta

5. Which of the following politicians' vocal opposition to British control over Canadian foreign affairs made Canadian sovereignty a major issue during the First World War?

   A. Louis Riel

   B. Pierre Trudeau

   C. Henri Bourassa

   D. Sir Clifford Sifton

6. The principle of equality and mutual respect among Canada's ethnic groups is called

   A. diversity

   B. tolerance

   C. integration

   D. multiculturalism

7. Which of the following groups has greeted Canada's official policies of bilingualism and multiculturalism with the **most** hostility and skepticism?

   A. The Québécois

   B. Western Canadians

   C. First Nations peoples

   D. English-speaking Canadians

Use the following information to answer the next two questions.

Society I	Includes various groups of different cultures, religions, and ethnicities that are interdependent
Society II	Includes one culture and religion for all members of the society. Diversity is not promoted or accepted
Society III	Includes different minority ethnic and cultural groups that have sovereign decision-making power over some issues within the confines of the federal government
Society IV	Includes two different cultures that dominate the political and social landscape of the country

8. Which of the given societies would **best** be described as pluralistic?

A. Society I

B. Society II

C. Society III

D. Society IV

9. Which of the given societies is the **best** example of a multination model?

A. Society I

B. Society II

C. Society III

D. Society IV

ANSWERS AND SOLUTIONS—PRACTICE QUESTIONS

1. A	**3. C**	**5. C**	**7. A**	**9. C**
2. B	**4. C**	**6. D**	**8. A**	

1. **A**

   Canadians had marched off to war in 1914 as proud subjects of the British Empire. Their primary motivation was imperialism—devotion to the British Empire. During the war, they developed a new sense of Canadian nationalism and stopped thinking of themselves as British subjects and colonials (inhabitants of a colony). They started to regard Canada as a nation in its own right instead of thinking of it as a mere colony of Britain.

   The experience of war greatly strengthened Canadian nationalism (devotion to Canada); it certainly did not causc it to disappear. During the war years, Canadians worked closely with the British and our servicemen spent considerable periods of time in Britain. During this time, they came to think of themselves as North Americans rather than as Europeans. The wartime experience did not fundamentally change Canada's relationship with the monarchy; Canada remains a constitutional monarchy today.

2. **B**

   The term *national consciousness* refers to a people's awareness of their nationhood. Having a national consciousness means a nation has a national identity and shares a common devotion to the nation (nationalism). The fact that Canadian soldiers in 1939 (the Second World War), 1950 (the Korean War), and 1999 (NATO's Operation Allied Force against the former Yugoslavia) were proud to fight for Canada indicates they had developed a sense of nationalism during and after the First World War.

   None of the other factors explain the rise of Canadian nationalism during and immediately after the First World War. For example, immigration levels of British citizens moving to Canada remained relatively high during the interwar years of 1919 to 1939 and would not help to explain the rise of Canadian nationalism and the decline of devotion to Britain during those years.

3. **C**

   The term *sovereignty* refers to the independent decision-making power of a state or nation.

   The term *sovereignty* can refer to the status or authority of a sovereign (a king or queen) or the status or authority of a royal family (royalty)—but not to the royal family itself. Nationalism is an important ingredient in the maintenance of national sovereignty, but *nationalism* is not synonymous with *sovereignty*. A sovereign nation must effectively control its national territory and national borders to be sovereign, but the term does not refer to territory or borders per se.

4. **C**

   Louis Riel worked closely with the federal government to come to an agreement regarding the entry of Manitoba into Canadian Confederation.

   Louis Riel did not have influence on the entry of British Columbia, Alberta, or Saskatchewan into Confederation.

5. C

Henri Bourassa was vehemently opposed to the fact that the decision for Canada to enter the First World War was made by Britain, not Canada. As a result, many people in Canada (in particular those of French descent) called for greater Canadian sovereignty.

Neither Louis Riel nor Pierre Trudeau were politicians during the First World War.
Sir Clifford Sifton did not share Bourassa's strong opposition.

6. D

***Multiculturalism* can be defined as the principle of equality and mutual respect among Canada's ethnic groups.**

The term *diversity* means being varied or exhibiting variety. *Tolerance* refers to a willingness to accept people who have opinions or customs that differ from one's own. *Integration* is the process of mixing an ethnic or racial group with an existing community.

7. A

The Québécois (French-speaking Quebecers) have tended to view official bilingualism as a scheme to assimilate francophone Quebecers by encouraging them to speak English. Many of them believe the policy endangers the survival of the French language in North America. Similarly, the Québécois perceive multiculturalism as a means of reducing Quebecers' status as one of Canada's two founding peoples. They argue that official multiculturalism is an attempt to label francophone Quebecers as just another ethnic group in Canada.

Western Canadians have given official bilingualism mixed reviews, but multiculturalism has been a very popular policy in the culturally diverse West.
First Nations peoples want more recognition than is afforded by official bilingualism and multiculturalism, but they are not as suspicious of these policies as are francophone Quebecers.
English-speaking Canadians tend to regard bilingualism as essential for maintaining national unity and have generally embraced multiculturalism.

8. A

In a pluralistic society, various cultures, ethnicities, and religions live together and are interdependent, as described in Society I.

None of the other societies describe this type of situation. Rather, they describe varying levels of segregation of different cultures within society, which is contradictory to the idea of pluralism.

9. C

In the multination model, government systems are set up in order to allow a minority to have a form of self-government and to form a majority in that area. Society III describes a situation in which different cultural minorities have some autonomy within the confines of a larger nation.

None of the other societies describe this type of situation.

UNIT TEST—RELATED ISSUE 4

1. Which of the following men was one of the Fathers of Confederation?

A. Louis-Hippolyte Lafontaine

B. John A. Macdonald

C. Robert Baldwin

D. Pierre Trudeau

Use the following information to answer the next two questions.

Action I	Patriated the Canadian Constitution
Action II	Officially recognized multiculturalism in Canada
Action III	Introduced the Official Languages Act

2. The person responsible for each of the given actions while he was prime minister of Canada is

A. Jean Chrétien

B. Pierre Trudeau

C. Henri Bourassa

D. Brian Mulroney

3. Which of the following actions could correctly be added to the given list?

A. Enacted conscription

B. Enacted the War Measures Act

C. Introduced the Meech Lake Accord

D. Introduced the Charlottetown Agreement

4. The basis for the Quiet Revolution in Canada was a

A. feeling of unity between Quebec and the federal government

B. belief in the need to use violent means to achieve Quebec sovereignty

C. desire of Quebecers to feel a greater sense of devotion to Canada than to Quebec

D. desire for autonomy and recognition for Quebec as being distinct from the rest of Canada

Use the following information to answer the next three questions.

Speaker I	My Canada encompasses many different religions, races, cultures, and traditions all living together with a common goal—the promotion of our great country. When people feel that their differences are celebrated and respected, there is no need for separation or self-determination for any cultural group.
Speaker II	Allowing distinct cultural groups to have some control over their own affairs is essential if we are to have a multicultural society in which all groups are happy and satisfied. We must allow for some separation of governments along cultural lines.
Speaker III	Canada must spend less time worrying about which culture has its feelings hurt now and worry about our role in international affairs. Our democracy, the wealth of our country, and our commitment to justice puts us in a position to set an example for the rest of the world.
Speaker IV	It is unrealistic for Canada to think it can survive forever without more involvement with those around us, specifically the United States and Mexico. As the European Union gains strength, the rest of the world must consider regional agreements that cross current lines of sovereignty.

5. The speaker who is **most supportive** of pluralism as a future for Canada is

A. Speaker I

B. Speaker II

C. Speaker III

D. Speaker IV

6. Agreements such as NAFTA would **most likely** be supported by which of the speakers?

A. Speaker I

B. Speaker II

C. Speaker III

D. Speaker IV

7. The speaker who would **most likely** be supportive of First Nations self-governance is

A. Speaker I

B. Speaker II

C. Speaker III

D. Speaker IV

8. The promotion of Canadian unity is **best** represented by the

A. Maple Leaf

B. national anthem

C. Canadian Constitution

D. Charter of Rights and Freedoms

9. The organization responsible for regulating how much exposure Canadians get to Canadian content in the media is the

A. CBC

B. CRTC

C. RCMP

D. DND/CF

Use the following information to answer the next two questions.

Major Points Involved in First Nations Self-Determination	
Point I	Establishment of independent communities through treaties
Point II	Control over day-to-day affairs
Point III	Maintenance of the reserve system
Point IV	Stronger ties to the federal government

10. Which of the given points does **not** belong on this list?

A. Point I

B. Point II

C. Point III

D. Point IV

11. Which of the following areas would **not** be included in point II?

A. Education

B. Health care

C. Judicial systems

D. National defence

12. The Métis Settlements Act of 1990 in Alberta legislated

- **A.** local self-governance for eight Alberta Métis settlements
- **B.** federal government control of eight Alberta Métis settlements
- **C.** official provincial government protection of Métis culture in Alberta
- **D.** resolution between Métis and First Nations over land claims in Alberta

Use the following information to answer the next question.

> "The future of this country is not only in Ontario and Quebec but out West. The vast lands and hard-working people there are a resource that will be invaluable to the well-being of Canada. More great people are needed to populate this country and make it all that it can be. Let's bring them here in droves and make this country great!"

13. The speaker in the given quotation is **most likely**

- **A.** Louis Riel
- **B.** Pierre Trudeau
- **C.** Henri Bourassa
- **D.** Sir Clifford Sifton

14. The two people who initiated responsible government in Canada were

- **A.** Jean Chrétien and Pierre Trudeau
- **B.** Robert Baldwin and Pierre Trudeau
- **C.** Louis-Hippolyte Lafontaine and Jean Chrétien
- **D.** Louis-Hippolyte Lafontaine and Robert Baldwin

Use the following information to answer the next three questions.

Speaker I	Cultural diversity is what makes Canada unique in the world. Around the globe, people see Canada as an oasis of tolerance and understanding—that is what Canadians should embrace as their identity.
Speaker II	To not support and promote the existence of both French and English as equals in Canada would be to ignore our history. We must find a way to make sure both languages stay at the forefront of Canada's identity without tearing the country in two.
Speaker III	Respect for the French language outside of Quebec is virtually non-existent. All Canadians saw that most people did not feel it was part of their identity in 1990 and again in 1992, when the rest of the country refused to acknowledge the uniqueness of French society.
Speaker IV	What does it mean to be Canadian? Who knows? We have so many different races, cultures, and religions, each refusing to drop the hyphen and just be Canadian. Our identity is something that is impossible to define or, therefore, to be proud of.

15. The speaker who is **most supportive** of Canada's pluralistic society is

A. Speaker I

B. Speaker II

C. Speaker III

D. Speaker IV

16. Which of the following people would **most likely** hold or have held an opinion closest to that of Speaker III?

A. Louis Riel

B. Jean Chrétien

C. Pierre Trudeau

D. René Lévesque

17. Which two speakers hold the **most different** opinions of Canada's multicultural society?

A. Speakers I and II

B. Speakers I and IV

C. Speakers II and III

D. Speakers III and IV

18. Which of the following actions would the Canadian government **most likely** take if it was to encourage further North American integration in the economy?

A. Reduce restrictions on foreign ownership in Canada

B. Eliminate restrictions on Canadian content in the media

C. Introduce tariffs on goods imported from the United States

D. Subsidize Canadian businesses that compete with the United States and Mexico

19. The **main** goal of the Indian Act when it was first enacted in 1876 was to

A. assimilate First Nations people into Canadian culture

B. establish self-determination for First Nations within Canada

C. solve land disputes between First Nations and the federal government

D. protect the unique cultural differences among different First Nations groups

ANSWERS AND SOLUTIONS—UNIT TEST

1. B	**5. A**	**9. B**	**13. D**	**17. B**
2. B	**6. D**	**10. D**	**14. D**	**18. A**
3. B	**7. B**	**11. D**	**15. A**	**19. A**
4. D	**8. A**	**12. A**	**16. D**	

1. B

John A. Macdonald was the first prime minister of Canada after the signing of the British North America Act in 1867. His work, along with that of many other men, to create the Dominion of Canada made him one of the Fathers of Confederation.

None of the other men were part of the group that formed the Fathers of Confederation.

2. B

Each of the given actions was taken by Pierre Trudeau when he was prime minister of Canada.

Neither Jean Chrétien nor Brian Mulroney took these actions while he was prime minister. Henri Bourassa was never a prime minister of Canada.

3. B

While he was prime minister, Pierre Trudeau enacted the War Measures Act during the FLQ Crisis of 1970.

Trudeau was not responsible for the Meech Lake Accord, the Charlottetown Agreement, or conscription.

4. D

The Quiet Revolution of the 1960s in Canada was spurred by Jean Lesage and his desire for Quebec to be recognized as distinct from the rest of Canada. Lesage wanted Quebec to be given certain privileges based on its cultural uniqueness. This propelled the Quebec sovereignty movement into the national spotlight.

The Quiet Revolution was so named because violence was not promoted as a way to achieve change. Feelings of unity between Quebec and the federal government were weakened during the Quiet Revolution, and Quebecers were not encouraged to feel a greater sense of devotion to Canada, but to Quebec.

5. A

Pluralism is the acceptance and promotion of many different types of cultures, traditions, etc., within society. Speaker I clearly shows support for this type of society in Canada.

Speaker II is supportive of a multination model by which government systems are set up to allow a minority to have a form of self-government, such as the Quebec provincial government in Canada. Speaker III calls for Canada to be a global leader in the future. Speaker IV believes North American integration is important to Canada's future.

6. D

Speaker IV discusses the importance of North American integration to allow Canada to compete on a global scale. Agreements such as NAFTA are examples of this type of integration.

None of the other speakers presents opinions that suggests he or she would support or disagree with agreements like NAFTA.

7. B

Speaker II discusses the multination model by which government systems are set up to allow a minority group to have a form of self-government, such as the Quebec provincial government in Canada. Because of this belief, this speaker would also likely support First Nations self-governance.

None of the other speakers presents opinions that indicate likely support for First Nations self-governance.

8. A

The Maple Leaf is useful in promoting Canadian unity because it is something that is recognized by all Canadians and many people in other countries. It is something that all Canadians share and feel connected to.

Although the national anthem is an important part of Canadian unity, fewer Canadians can recite the words to the anthem than can recognize the Maple Leaf. The Charter of Rights and Freedoms is part of the Canadian Constitution. These documents are important parts of Canada's identity but have less impact on Canadian unity than does the flag, as Canadians do not identify with these two documents the way they do with the Maple Leaf.

9. B

The CRTC (Canadian Radio-television and Telecommunications Commission) is the body that regulates how much Canadian content is in all types of media in Canada.

The CBC (Canadian Broadcasting Corporation) is the television and radio broadcasting organization that promotes Canadian talent and issues across the country, but it has no regulating powers. Neither the RCMP (Royal Canadian Mounted Police) nor the DND/CF (Department of National Defence and Canadian Forces) has any relation to the Canadian media.

10. D

Through self-determination, First Nations people want to loosen the ties their communities have to the federal government and gain more control over their own affairs.

Points I, II, and III are correct.

11. D

National defence is not something that would be under the control of First Nations government systems; it would be left to the Canadian federal government.

Health care, education, and the judicial system are all areas that would be controlled by a First Nations government system.

12. A

Among other things, the Métis Settlements Act established the only form of Métis government in Canada through local self-governance in the eight Métis settlements in Alberta.

The act did not give the federal government control over the settlements, establish cultural protection by the provincial government, or settle land claims disputes between Métis and First Nations people.

13. D

Sir Clifford Sifton was a Canadian politician who was known for his support of Western Canadian issues. He believed that massive immigration was important for Canada's development.

None of the other men listed would likely have had this opinion, as each had a different focus during his political career.

14. D

Louis-Hippolyte Lafontaine and Robert Baldwin initiated responsible government in Canada during the late 1800s.

Responsible government already existed in Canada by the time Jean Chrétien and Pierre Trudeau entered Canadian politics.

15. A

Speaker I describes how Canada encompasses many different cultures. The speaker also describes how there is tolerance and acceptance of these differences, which is what it means to have a pluralistic society.

Speaker II is supportive of bilingualism but does not suggest support for many different cultures. Speaker III believes the separation of French and English is important and does not support pluralism.Speaker IV feels that pluralism is detrimental to Canada's identity.

16. D

René Lévesque was the premier of Quebec from 1976 to 1985, and he was supportive of sovereignty for Quebec.

None of the other men listed was supportive of separation for Quebec and would not likely have agreed with Speaker III.

17. B

Speaker I believes multiculturalism to be beneficial to Canada's identity and reputation around the world, while Speaker IV suggests multiculturalism has caused a crisis of identity in Canada.

Speakers II and III address issues surrounding bilingualism rather than multiculturalism.

18. A

Reducing restrictions on foreign ownership in Canada would allow for businesses from other countries to have more of a presence in Canada and would encourage the integration of the Canadian economy with economies of other countries.

Introducing tariffs and subsidizing businesses are both protectionist policies that would limit integration of economies. Eliminating restrictions on Canadian media content would have more of an effect on the cultural integration of Canada with other countries.

19. A

Under the Indian Act of 1876, the federal government legislated its right to make decisions about First Nations people and the lands they inhabited. Through various laws, the government attempted to assimilate the First Nations people into Canadian culture.

The Act did not attempt to protect cultural differences, solve land disputes, or establish self-determination for First Nations people.

KEY Strategies for Success on Tests

TEST PREPARATION AND TEST-TAKING SKILLS

THINGS TO CONSIDER WHEN TAKING A TEST

It is normal to feel anxious before you write a test. You can manage this anxiety by

- Thinking positive thoughts. Imagine yourself doing well on the test.
- Making a conscious effort to relax by taking several slow, deep, controlled breaths. Concentrate on the air going in and out of your body.
- Before you begin the test, ask questions if you are unsure of anything.
- Jot down key words or phrases from any instructions your teacher gives you.
- Look over the entire test to find out the number and kinds of questions on the test.
- Read each question closely and reread if necessary.
- Pay close attention to key vocabulary words. Sometimes these are **bolded** or *italicized*, and they are usually important words in the question.
- If you are putting your answers on an answer sheet, mark your answers carefully. Always print clearly. If you wish to change an answer, erase the mark completely and then ensure your final answer is darker than the one you have erased.
- Use highlighting to note directions, key words, and vocabulary that you find confusing or that are important to answering the question.
- Double-check to make sure you have answered everything before handing in your test.

When taking tests, students often overlook the easy words. Failure to pay close attention to these words can result in an incorrect answer. One way to avoid this is to be aware of these words and to underline, circle, or highlight them while you are taking the test.

Even though some words are easy to understand, they can change the meaning of the entire question, so it is important that you pay attention to them. Here are some examples.

all	always	most likely	probably	best	not
difference	usually	except	most	unlikely	likely

Example

1. During the race, Susan is **most likely** feeling

A. sad

B. weak

C. scared

D. determined

HELPFUL STRATEGIES FOR ANSWERING MULTIPLE-CHOICE QUESTIONS

A multiple-choice question gives you some information, and then asks you to select an answer from four choices. Each question has one correct answer. The other answers are distractors, which are incorrect. Below are some strategies to help you when answering multiple-choice questions.

- Quickly skim through the entire test. Find out how many questions there are and plan your time accordingly.
- Read and reread questions carefully. Underline key words and try to think of an answer before looking at the choices.
- If there is a graphic, look at the graphic, read the question, and go back to the graphic. Then, you may want to underline the important information from the question.
- Carefully read the choices. Read the question first and then each answer that goes with it.
- When choosing an answer, try to eliminate those choices that are clearly wrong or do not make sense.
- Some questions may ask you to select the best answer. These questions will always include words like *best*, *most appropriate*, or *most likely*. All of the answers will be correct to some degree, but one of the choices will be better than the others in some way. Carefully read all four choices before choosing the answer you think is the best.
- If you do not know the answer, or if the question does not make sense to you, it is better to guess than to leave it blank.
- Do not spend too much time on any one question. Make a mark (*) beside a difficult question and come back to it later. If you are leaving a question to come back to later, make sure you also leave the space on the answer sheet, if you are using one.
- Remember to go back to the difficult questions at the end of the test; sometimes clues are given throughout the test that will provide you with answers.
- Note any negative words like *no* or *not* and be sure your choice fits the question.
- Before changing an answer, be sure you have a very good reason to do so.
- Do not look for patterns on your answer sheet, if you are using one.

HELPFUL STRATEGIES FOR ANSWERING OPEN-RESPONSE QUESTIONS

A written response requires you to respond to a question or directive such as *explain*, *predict*, *list*, *describe*, *show your work*, *solve*, or *calculate*. In preparing for open-response tasks you may wish to:

- Read and reread the question carefully.
- Recognize and pay close attention to directing words such as *explain*, *show your work*, and *describe*.
- Underline key words and phrases that indicate what is required in your answer, such as *explain*, *estimate*, *answer*, *calculate*, or *show your work*.
- Write down rough, point-form notes regarding the information you want to include in your answer.
- Think about what you want to say and organize information and ideas in a coherent and concise manner within the time limit you have for the question.
- Be sure to answer every part of the question that is asked.
- Include as much information as you can when you are asked to explain your thinking.
- Include a picture or diagram if it will help to explain your thinking.
- Try to put your final answer to a problem in a complete sentence to be sure it is reasonable.
- Reread your response to ensure you have answered the question.
- Think: does your answer make sense
- Listen: does it sound right?
- Use appropriate subject vocabulary and terms in your response.

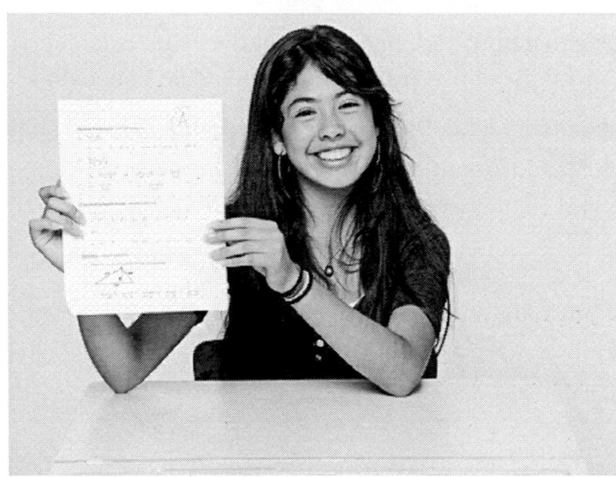

TEST PREPARATION COUNTDOWN

If you develop a plan for studying and test preparation, you will perform well on tests.

Here is a general plan to follow seven days before you write a test.

Countdown: 7 Days before the Test

1. Use "Finding Out About the Test" to help you make your own personal test preparation plan.
2. Review the following information:
   – areas to be included on the test
   – types of test items
   – general and specific test tips
3. Start preparing for the test at least 7 days before the test. Develop your test preparation plan and set time aside to prepare and study.

Countdown: 6, 5, 4, 3, 2 Days before the Test

4. Review old homework assignments, quizzes, and tests.
5. Rework problems on quizzes and tests to make sure you still know how to solve them.
6. Correct any errors made on quizzes and tests.
7. Review key concepts, processes, formulas, and vocabulary.
8. Create practice test questions for yourself and then answer them. Work out many sample problems.

Countdown: The Night before the Test

1. The night before the test is for final preparation, which includes reviewing and gathering material needed for the test before going to bed.
2. Most important is getting a good night's rest and knowing you have done everything possible to do well on the test.

Test Day

1. Eat a healthy and nutritious breakfast.
2. Ensure you have all the necessary materials.
3. Think positive thoughts: "I can do this." "I am ready." "I know I can do well."
4. Arrive at your school early so you are not rushing, which can cause you anxiety and stress.

SUMMARY OF HOW TO BE SUCCESSFUL DURING A TEST

You may find some of the following strategies useful for writing a test.

- Take two or three deep breaths to help you relax.
- Read the directions carefully and underline, circle, or highlight any important words.
- Look over the entire test to understand what you will need to do.
- Budget your time.
- Begin with an easy question, or a question you know you can answer correctly, rather than following the numerical question order of the test.
- If you cannot remember how to answer a question, try repeating the deep breathing and physical relaxation activities first. Then, move on to visualization and positive self-talk to get yourself going.
- When answering a question with graphics (pictures, diagrams, tables, or graphs), look at the question carefully.
    1. Read the title of the graphic and any key words.
    2. Read the test question carefully to figure out what information you need to find in the graphic.
    3. Go back to the graphic to find the information you need.
- Write down anything you remember about the subject on the reverse side of your test paper. This activity sometimes helps to remind you that you do know something and you are capable of writing the test.
- Look over your test when you have finished and double-check your answers to be sure you did not forget anything.

Practice Tests

PRACTICE TEST 1

Use the following information to answer the next two questions.

Speaker I	I reject nationalism. It is by nature intolerant and discriminatory. It defines the common good as a function of the ethnic group rather than of all the people, regardless of characteristics. A democratic government should stand for and encourage good citizenship, but never nationalism. Instead of nationalism, I believe in patriotism. Patriotism is the belief that the state must govern for the good of all the people within its boundaries.
Speaker II	The strongest kind of nationalism is based on ancestry and culture. This is the type of nationalism I carry in my heart. Even though my family has been in Canada for about a hundred years, I still identify most strongly with my ancestral culture. I love my ancestor's food, music, and traditions. I am proud to be a "hyphenated Canadian" who gives slightly more loyalty to her "blood nationality" than to her "passport nationality."
Speaker III	I am very nationalistic. Nationalism is important, but it must be nationalism based on reason rather than on emotion. What should bind people together as a nation is respect for the same laws and values.
Speaker IV	The nationalism I believe in is founded upon the sharing of a common language, territory, history, and folklore, as well as common customs. Any group of people that has these things in common must be a sovereign nation.

1. Which two speakers believe in civic nationalism?

A. Speakers I and III

B. Speakers II and III

C. Speakers II and IV

D. Speakers III and IV

2. Which speaker's brand of nationalism poses the **greatest** threat to national unity in Canada?

A. Speaker I

B. Speaker II

C. Speaker III

D. Speaker IV

Use the following information to answer the next question.

Foreign Policy Goals of a Particular Nation

Goal I	Achieve greater prestige in the international community by increasing our military might and developing weapons of mass destruction
Goal II	Seek every opportunity to expand our borders at the expense of neighbouring states
Goal III	Employ unfair trading practices and do business with nations that grossly violate human rights.
Goal IV	Participate only in United Nations operations and activities that directly serve our narrow national interests.

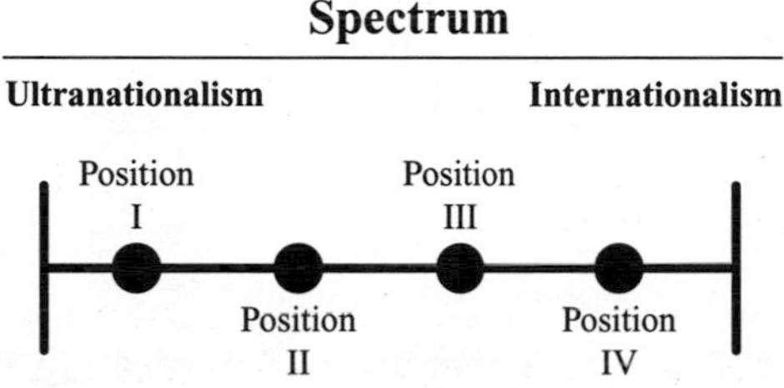

3. Which point on the given spectrum represents the foreign policy of this nation?

A. Position I

B. Position II

C. Position III

D. Position IV

Use the following information to answer the next question.

Criteria for Decision-Making

- Treaty links
- Geographic location
- Ideological like-mindedness
- Political and cultural affinity
- Stage of economic development

4. All of the given criteria would be **most carefully** considered by a nation when it

A. decides whether or not to send humanitarian aid to other nations

B. admits new member-states into nongovernmental organizations

C. forms voting groups in the United Nations General Assembly

D. chooses a location for an international conference

Use the following information to answer the next question.

> The [economic] collapse of 1929–1933 put an end to the high hopes for a shared prosperity which had marked the post-war years. Now, as world trade fell, each nation determined to hang on to what was left, and at any rate to keep its own trade intact. This was a policy of economic nationalism—a far cry from the economic internationalism of which President Wilson had dreamed.
>
> —from *The 20th* Century

5. Which of the following strategies is **inconsistent** with the policy of "economic nationalism" described in the given excerpt?

A. Negotiating multilateral trade agreements among nations

B. Erecting protectionist barriers to international commerce

C. Imposing quotas on imported goods

D. Increasing tariffs on foreign goods

6. Quebec separatists would **most likely** argue that the goal of creating an independent Quebec reflects a desire for

A. containment

B. appeasement

C. brinkmanship

D. self-determination

Use the following information to answer the next two questions.

At a public forum during a recent election campaign, four candidates were asked to respond to the following question:

Should Canada continue to trade with countries that have poor human rights records?

Candidate I
You should not mix economics with other nations' internal politics. Canadians want to enjoy the benefits of a growing economy. Canada must trade with nations that are willing to trade with us. International trade creates badly needed jobs for Canadians. If we refuse to trade with another nation, then other countries will simply step in and take advantage of the situation. Our corporations will lose valuable markets for their products.

Candidate II
Certainly international trade provides positive benefits for Canada, but equally important is the fact that our trade with other nations provides economic opportunity for people in other nations. We must continue to trade with nations that violate human rights because as their economic conditions improve, it is very likely that political reforms will follow. In the meantime, our government should continue to be involved in diplomatic efforts to promote respect for human rights.

Candidate III
Canada is recognized as an international role model because it places value on protecting human rights. We do not allow Canadian workers to be exploited in "sweatshop" factories or to be imprisoned for simply speaking out against the government. We have a double standard when we ignore these things happening in other nations. Canada needs to lead by example. We must not trade with nations that abuse the rights of their citizens.

Candidate IV
If Canada ends trade contacts with nations that demonstrate poor human rights records, we will lose any chance of pressuring those nations to change. The best policy is a balanced policy. Canadian trade ties with such nations should be maintained; however, our political leaders must make it clear that any expansion of trade will be directly linked to improved human rights records.

7. Which candidate **most clearly** places national interests ahead of international concerns?

- **A.** Candidate I
- **B.** Candidate II
- **C.** Candidate III
- **D.** Candidate IV

8. The human rights protection organization Amnesty International would **most strongly** support the position taken by

- **A.** Candidate I
- **B.** Candidate II
- **C.** Candidate III
- **D.** Candidate IV

9. Nationalists in some European nations express fear that the movement toward greater cooperation in western Europe threatens their

A. international trade positions

B. citizens' rights and freedoms

C. economic and cultural sovereignty

D. government funding for social programs

10. The **primary** goal of NAFTA is to achieve economic

A. security through nationalization

B. equality through sharing technologies

C. cooperation through closer trade links

D. prosperity through global competition

Use the following information to answer the next two questions.

Questions Posed to an Internationalist

I
Should Canada withdraw from the military alliances of NATO and NORAD?

II
Should Canadian soldiers continue to serve in international peacekeeping operations?

III
Should the Canadian government use economic and political pressure to punish nations that break international laws and/or violate human rights?

IV
Should Canada take a leadership role in organizing international efforts to end the production of weapons of war?

V
Should the Canadian government focus more on national concerns and less on international issues?

VI
Should Canada pursue more free trade agreements with other nations?

VII
Should the Canadian government reduce its spending on foreign assistance to developing nations?

11. An internationalist would **most likely** answer *yes* to which of the given questions?

A. I, II, VI, and VII

B. I, III, V, and VII

C. II, III, IV, and VI

D. II, IV, V, and VI

12. Which of the following sources of information would be **most useful** in answering question VI?

A. A report evaluating the successes and failures of the European Union and NAFTA

B. Statistics from the United Nations on global population growth rates and life expectancy trends

C. A report on the benefits of, and problems associated with, international sporting events such as the Olympics

D. Statistics from the Canadian government detailing the amount of money spent on national defence for each of the last ten years

Use the following information to answer the next question.

During the 1996 presidential election campaign in the United States, a candidate for the leadership of the Republican party promised to dissolve the North American Free Trade Agreement and end government spending on foreign assistance.

13. The promises of the candidate indicate a belief that American foreign policy should shift toward

A. increased isolationism in the global community

B. greater support for global human rights protection

C. increased involvement in settling international disputes

D. greater reliance on global collective security to resolve disputes

Use the following information to answer the next question.

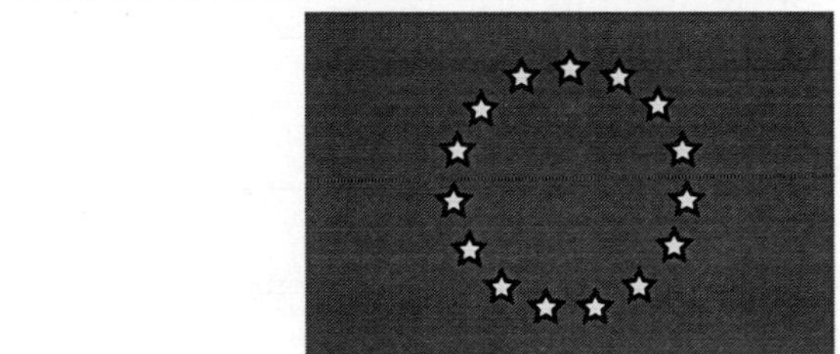

The flag of the European Union—each star represents a member nation.

14. The arrangement of stars on the flag symbolizes European Union efforts to

A. create unity by promoting economic cooperation among member nations

B. isolate member nations from international economic relations

C. create a powerful and aggressive military alliance

D. eliminate the need for the United Nations

Use the following information to answer the next question.

In January 1992, the Secretary General of the United Nations drew up a plan for reform. A central part of this plan was called the "Agenda for Peace." Under this agenda, the business of making and keeping peace has four stages:

Stage I Preventative diplomacy aims to stop disputes before they start.

Stage II Peacemaking is action taken to stop conflicts after they start.

Stage III Peacekeeping means putting people in the field to keep warring parties apart.

Stage IV Peace building involves putting structures in place to help keep the peace and stop wars from restarting.

—from *Canada and the World*

15. When the United Nations deals with conflicts at Stage I, the intention is to avoid the

A. attention of the media

B. high cost of armed conflict

C. involvement of superpowers

D. use of international negotiations

16. An internationalist would react positively to a decision made by Canada to

A. withdraw from membership in the World Trade Organization

B. purchase long-range bombers for its armed forces

C. reduce immigration quotas for political refugees

D. increase spending on foreign assistance projects

Use the following information to answer the next question.

An American poster from the Second World War

—from *Persuasive Images*

17. Two purposes of this poster were to

A. raise funds for the war effort and maintain citizen morale

B. express concern for the financial costs of war and promote racial tolerance

C. encourage antiwar sentiment and oppose the United States' entry into the war

D. provide information about victories and force an immediate German surrender

18. After the First World War, the creation of new nations in Europe reflected a belief that

A. the spread of democracy could threaten traditional European political beliefs

B. competition among nations would reduce the probability of future war

C. distinct ethnic groups should have the right to self-determination

D. another major European war was likely to occur within 20 years

Use the following information to answer the next two questions.

Prague is invaded

MARCH 15

Adolf Hitler took the Czech Sudetenland six months ago—now he has swallowed up the rest of Czechoslovakia. Hitler entered Prague, the Czech capital, today and installed himself in Hradzin Castle, the ancient palace of the Bohemian kings. The reception the German army has received is, however, in striking contrast to the tremendous welcome given to them in the Sudetenland and in Austria. In Prague, the crowds wept and courageously sang the national anthem as they were forced to salute the invading Nazi soldiers.

—from *The Illustrated History of the 20th* Century

19. The writer indicates that, when compared with previous Nazi territorial expansions, the invasion of Prague

A. was not supported by the people affected

B. was supported by other European nations

C. prevented an attack upon German territory

D. required the use of violent military confrontation

20. The given event demonstrates a consequence of Great Britain's decision to deal with German aggression through a foreign policy of

A. détente

B. isolationism

C. containment

D. appeasement

Use the following information to answer the next two questions.

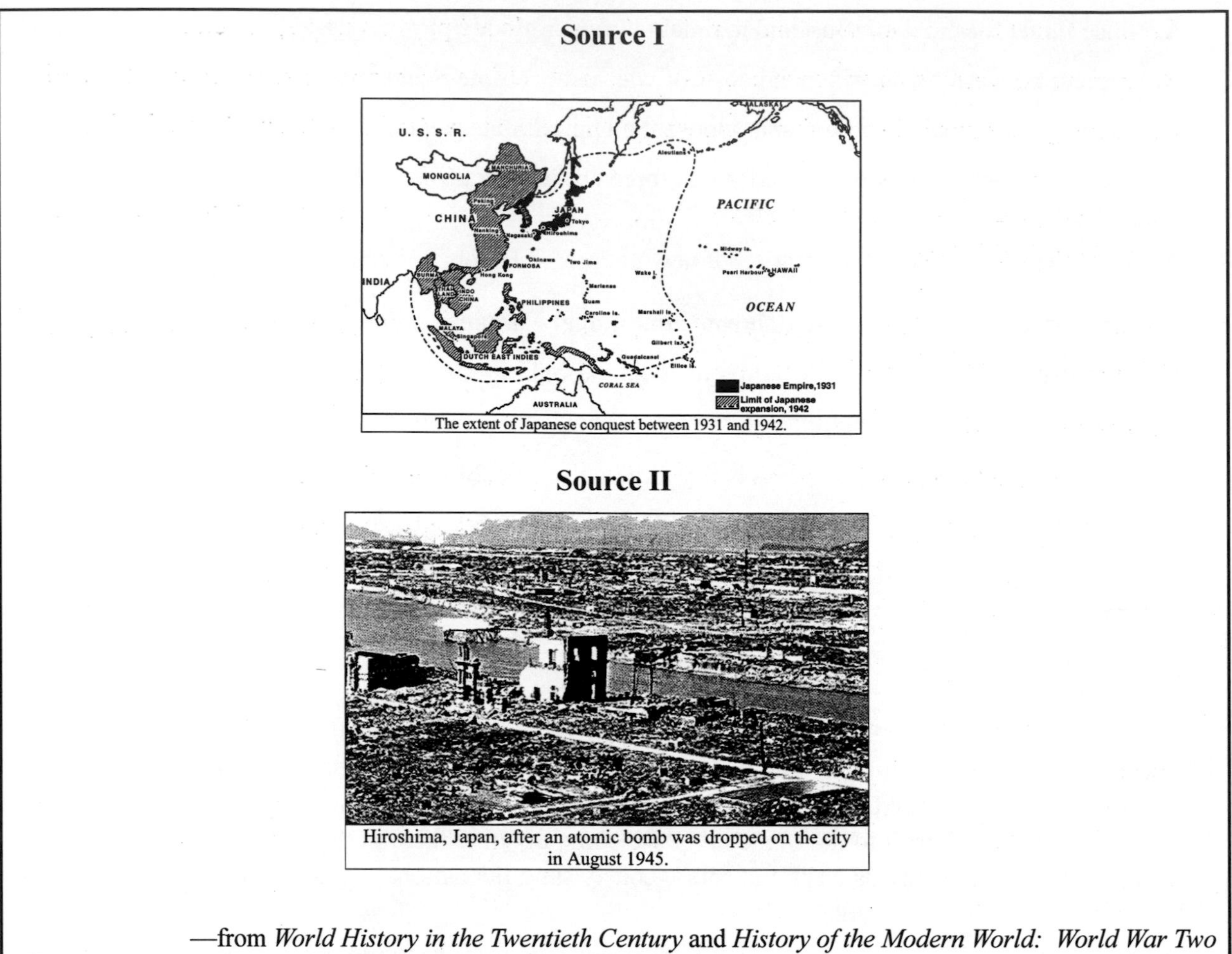

Source I

The extent of Japanese conquest between 1931 and 1942.

Source II

Hiroshima, Japan, after an atomic bomb was dropped on the city in August 1945.

—from *World History in the Twentieth Century* and *History of the Modern World: World War Two*

21. The Japanese undertook the territorial expansion illustrated in Source I **primarily** as a means of

- **A.** restoring peace to an area of Asia that had been ravaged by war
- **B.** preventing Western nations from establishing colonies in Asia
- **C.** liberating Asians from the brutal control of dictatorships
- **D.** ensuring Japanese control of essential natural resources

22. Taken together, the given sources provide evidence to support the generalization that

- **A.** wars are often started by nations seeking revenge for past defeats
- **B.** warfare in the 20th century was more humane than warfare in earlier times
- **C.** citizens may suffer serious consequences when their nation chooses to act aggressively
- **D.** differing military methods may be used to liberate ethnic groups living under the control of foreign rulers

23. One of the **main** goals of Amnesty International is to

A. ensure that the fundamental human rights of all people are preserved and protected

B. pressure governments and corporations to adhere to stricter environmental protection standards

C. lobby governments in an effort to convince nations to adopt foreign policies of isolationism and neutrality

D. encourage the reduction of economic barriers between nations so that transnational corporations can invest globally

24. Despite China's record regarding human rights, many Canadian activists for human rights support continued trade with China because they believe that Canada

A. has a human rights record that is no better than China's record

B. does not see human rights issues as being as important as economic issues

C. treats China differently than it does other nations that violate human rights

D. can influence political reforms in China by maintaining close trade relations

25. The European Union originated through the efforts of Member States to

A. remove borders between Member States

B. create a western European nuclear military force

C. improve environmental conditions across Europe

D. encourage better trade relations among Member States

Use the following information to answer the next question.

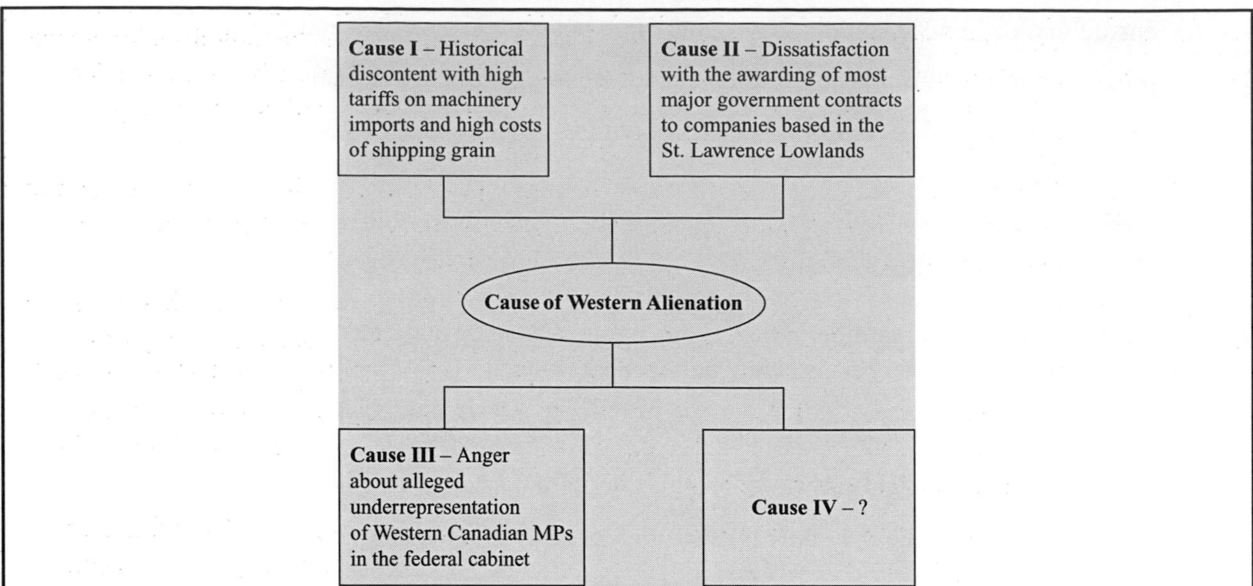

26. Which of the following causes would **best** complete the given diagram?

A. Resentment of the National Energy Program
B. Hostility toward the policy of multiculturalism
C. Dissatisfaction with Canada's immigration policy
D. Anger about provincial government cutbacks in health care and education

Use the following information to answer the next question.

Central domination has gradually weakened the sense of partnership and provincial equality that allowed Confederation to occur and flourish in the hearts and minds of Canadians everywhere. One manifestation of the hinterland anguish was a comment made by Newfoundland premier Clyde Wells in the early spring of 1990 that the earnings of Newfoundlanders (then only fifty-six per cent of the national average) had risen only three percentage points in twenty-six years.
"At that rate," he complained, "it would take us six hundred years to reach the national average."

—from *Inside Outer Canada*

27. The given passage suggests Canada's national unity is weakened by

A. regional diversity
B. misleading statistics
C. disparities within Canada
D. attempts at provincial equalization

Use the following information to answer the next two questions.

Speaker I	The world shares a sentimental approval of Canada—Mounties, biculturalism, tolerance, racial equality, slightly boring decency—that independence for Quebec would undermine. If tolerant Canada cannot share power across a linguistic divide, what hope is there for more bitterly divided societies?
Speaker II	Canada is one of the few societies that does not emphasize uniformity. That is a good thing because a society that emphasizes uniformity is one that creates intolerance and hate. Other countries should follow Canada's example in this regard.
Speaker III	Canada has created harmony and cooperation among ethnic groups, and it must take this experience to the world because there is yet to be such an example of harmony and cooperation among ethnic groups in other countries. There is hope for the human race if countries such as South Africa, Rwanda, and Bosnia can become more like Canada. If more nations followed Canada's path, inter-racial strife, civil war, and ethnic cleansing would become things of the past.
Speaker IV	The ideal society is one in which several different peoples can peacefully and interdependently exist in a single territory. If Canada's ethnic and linguistic groups can continue to collaborate at the hub of a truly pluralistic state, Canada will become the envied seat of a form of federalism that belongs to tomorrow's world. Canadian federalism is a brilliant prototype for the moulding of tomorrow's global civilization. I hope that every nation will adopt it.

28. All four speakers praise Canada for being a

A. federal state

B. plural society

C. multiracial country

D. bicultural community

29. All four speakers would **probably** support Canada's continued existence as a country through the cultivation of

A. bigotry

B. civic nationalism

C. ethnic segregation

D. cultural uniformity

Use the following information to answer the next two questions.

Statement I	Louis XVI's personal weaknesses magnified the inherent weaknesses of absolutism. Ordinary people came to see that it was foolish for the fate of the nation to depend on the decision-making capability of one individual. When the king called for a meeting of the Estates-General in 1788, commoners began to demand a separation of powers and a more representative form of government.
Statement II	France's hierarchical class structure had become a hindrance by 1789. By then the French people had realized that talent is wasted whenever an individual's destiny is fixed at the time of his birth. On the eve of the revolution, the majority of people in France wanted one's ability to count for more than one's parentage. This majority demanded the abolition of the privileges of the Second Estate.
Statement III	The finances of France were in a sorry state by 1789. The treasury had been depleted by France's costly intervention in the American War of Independence. The government created unrest when it fell behind in the payment of wages to officials, civil servants, and soldiers.
Statement IV	The philosophers set the stage for the French Revolution by convincing ordinary Frenchmen to adopt a whole new way of thinking. The Enlightenment was a revolution in ideas that laid the foundation for a revolution in actions. The Enlightenment was the birthplace of the modern mind.

30. Which statement refers to a social cause of the French Revolution?

A. Statement I

B. Statement II

C. Statement III

D. Statement IV

31. Which statement refers to an economic cause of the French Revolution?

A. Statement I

B. Statement II

C. Statement III

D. Statement IV

Use the following information to answer the next two questions.

Speaker I	We must enhance our influence in the Balkans. Furthermore, we must prevent any further Austrian expansion into southeastern Europe. This war presents us with the real possibility of acquiring control of the Dardanelles and warm-water ports in the Mediterranean. Finally, we will attempt to annex Galicia and Bukovina and eliminate the troublesome Ukrainian nationalist organizations in those two Austrian crown lands.
Speaker II	Our primary objective in the war is to obtain our irredentist claims; we must acquire the Austrian borderlands that are inhabited by members of our nationality. Our secondary objective is to acquire additional territories in Africa and on the other side of the Adriatic. By expanding our empire, we will achieve the status of a great power.
Speaker III	We must avenge our humiliation by Germany in the last war. In doing so, we will recapture the lost provinces of Alsace and Lorraine. Ultimately, we seek to permanently eliminate Germany as a threat to the security of our nation.
Speaker IV	Our primary goal in this war is to counteract German aspirations of domination. Our secondary aims are to liberate German-occupied territories, seize Germany's overseas colonies, and maintain our dominance of the high seas.

32. Which speaker states Italy's objectives in the First World War?

A. Speaker I

B. Speaker II

C. Speaker III

D. Speaker IV

33. Which of the speakers describes revenge and national security as motivation for its foreign policy and involvement in international agreements?

A. Speaker I

B. Speaker II

C. Speaker III

D. Speaker IV

Use the following information to answer the next two questions.

Image I

A propaganda poster celebrating a bountiful harvest.
Posters such as this were commonly used in Stalin's Soviet Union.
—from *Persuasive Images*

Image II

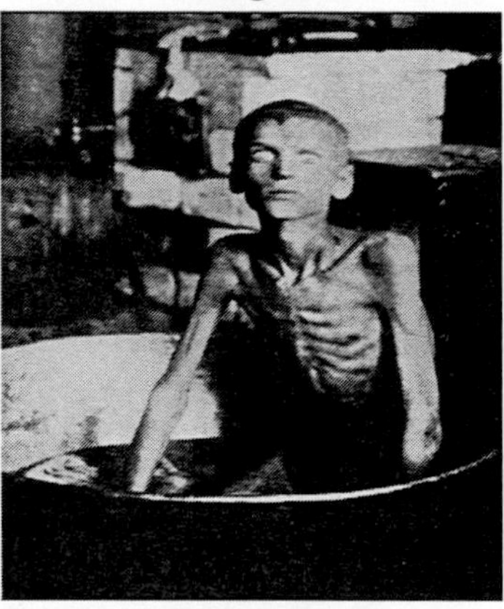

A child suffering from starvation.
A common sight in Stalin's Soviet Union.

34. The poster in Image I was intended to

A. praise business owners for making sound decisions

B. encourage public support for Soviet agricultural reforms

C. promote foreign investment in Soviet agricultural industries

D. prevent private landowners from selling land to the Soviet government

35. Which of the following concepts are contrasted by Image I and Image II?

A. Urban and rural lifestyles in Stalin's Soviet Union

B. Life in Tsarist Russia and life in Stalin's Soviet Union

C. The ideal and the reality of collectivization in Stalin's Soviet Union

D. Communist and anti-communist views of industrialization in Stalin's Soviet Union

36. The term *national self-determination* refers to

A. a nation's ability to encourage nationalism among its citizens

B. an act of aggression by one nation to take over another nation

C. the ability of a nation to govern itself without outside influence

D. the permission given to citizens of a nation to make decisions for themselves

Use the following information to answer the next question.

—from *The Edmonton Journal*, February 19, 2008, pg. A14

37. Which of the following statements give the **main** point of this cartoon?

A. Stephen Harper was unable to stop the independence movement in Kosovo and will be unable to prevent Quebec separation in Canada.

B. The events that led to Kosovo's independence are the same as those that fuel the Quebec independence movement.

C. Stephen Harper's political career is dependent on the decisions made about the Quebec separatist question.

D. Canada's recognition of a sovereign Kosovo could lead to increased support for a sovereign Quebec.

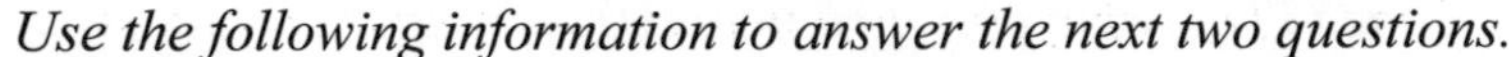
Use the following information to answer the next two questions.

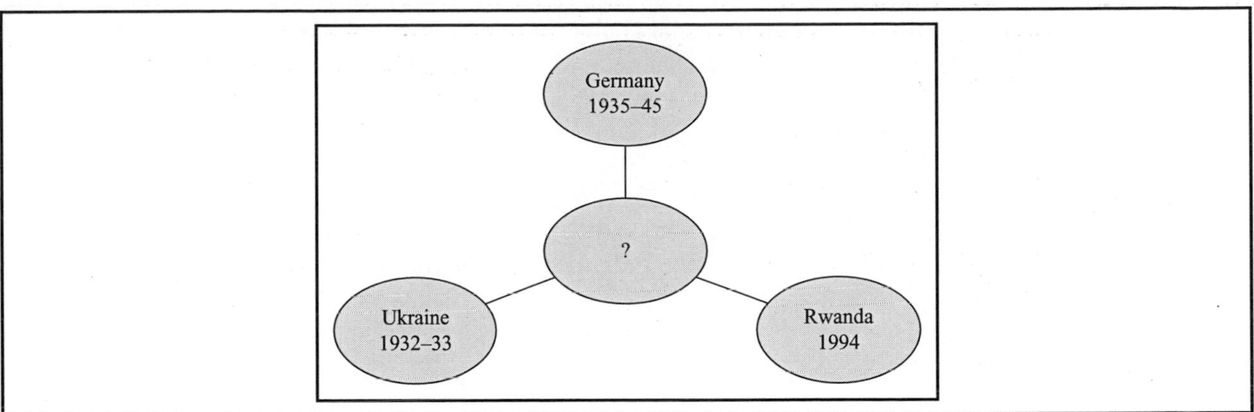

38. Which of the following titles could complete the given diagram?

A. Examples of Countries in Which Independence Was Gained as a Result of War

B. Examples of Countries in Which Genocide Was a Result of Ultranationalism

C. Examples of Countries in Which Violence Was a Result of Decolonization

D. Examples of Countries in Which Ultranationalism Resulted in Civil War

39. Which of the following places and dates could be added to the given diagram?

A. Soviet Union, 1991

B. France, 1995

C. Kosovo, 1996 to 1999

D. Canada, 1999

40. Each of the following groups is considered an institution that promotes Canada's national identity **except**

A. the CBC

B. the RCMP

C. the Bloc Québécois

D. Canada's peacekeepers

41. The CRTC is responsible for

A. establishing Canada's foreign policies

B. regulation of foreign investment in Canada

C. regulation of Canadian content in the media

D. providing security to Canada's political leaders

Use the following information to answer the next two questions.

"The federal government will unveil controversial changes to the Indian Act today in a move that is already being criticized by aboriginal leaders. The federal government has struggled for decades to make changes to the Act. Jean Chrétien tried to repeal it when he was Indian affairs minister in 1969, but failed in the face of opposition from First Nations leaders."

—from *http://www.cbc.ca/canada/story/2002/06/14/firstnations_bill020614.html*

42. The effort made by Jean Chrétien to repeal the Indian Act, as mentioned in the given quotation, was known as the

A. Métis Settlements Act

B. Indian Accord

C. White Paper

D. Red Book

43. The organization of First Nations leaders that was instrumental in the defeat of Chrétien's efforts as described in the given quotation was the

A. Assembly of First Nations

B. First Nations Confederacy

C. National Indian Brotherhood

D. Congress of Aboriginal Peoples

44. Which of the following accomplishments was achieved by Louis-Hippolyte Lafontaine?

A. The passing of the British North American Act

B. The establishment of responsible government in Canada

C. Leading the Métis resistance against the government in 1885

D. Establishing French and English as official languages in Canada

Use the following information to answer the next three questions.

Four Situations	
Situation I	A Francophone woman enrols her children in a French immersion school but speaks French at home
Situation II	An immigrant volunteers at his previous country's booth at Edmonton's Heritage Fair
Situation III	Citizens work together to achieve independence for their nation
Situation IV	A soldier pledges loyalty and a willingness to die in combat representing Canada

45. Which of the given situations gives an example of the expression of patriotic nationalism?

A. Situation I

B. Situation II

C. Situation III

D. Situation IV

46. The expression of political nationalism is **best** exemplified by which situation?

A. Situation I

B. Situation II

C. Situation III

D. Situation IV

47. The **best** example of a person finding reconciliation between two nationalist loyalties is given in

A. Situation I

B. Situation II

C. Situation III

D. Situation IV

48. A nation-state is **best** described as

A. an independent country

B. a multinational organization

C. a group of people sharing a minority culture within a larger community

D. self-government by a specific cultural group within a sovereign country

49. An example of conflict between Québécois nationalism and Canadian nationalism is represented by

A. the Official Languages Act, 1969

B. Bill 101, 1977

C. the Charter of Rights and Freedoms, 1982

D. the Multiculturalism Act, 1988

ANSWERS AND SOLUTIONS—PRACTICE TEST 1

1. A	11. C	21. D	31. C	41. C
2. D	12. A	22. C	32. B	42. C
3. A	13. A	23. A	33. C	43. C
4. C	14. A	24. D	34. B	44. B
5. A	15. B	25. D	35. C	45. D
6. D	16. D	26. A	36. C	46. C
7. A	17. A	27. C	37. D	47. B
8. C	18. C	28. B	38. B	48. A
9. C	19. A	29. B	39. C	49. B
10. C	20. D	30. B	40. C	

1. A

Civic nationalism is the belief that what holds a nation together should be a common belief in the same values, rights, and laws—not language, culture, or ethnicity. Speakers I and III express support for this type of nationalism. This question requires careful thought because Speaker I appears, on the surface, to reject both brands of nationalism (ethnic and civic); however, it becomes apparent that what he or she calls "patriotism" is the same thing as "civic nationalism."

Speakers II and IV express support for ethnic nationalism (cultural nationalism) based on blood, ancestry, folklore, and heritage. The emotional ties of blood and ancestry are more important to them than the more abstract and rational ties of civic nationalism.

2. D

The greatest threat to Canada's national unity at the present time is Québécois nationalism (Québécois separatism). Only Speaker IV describes nationalism similar to this. In fact, Speaker IV suggests that any culturally distinct group should establish its own country. This is the main argument used by Quebec separatists to justify Quebec's secession from Canada.

The civic nationalism of speakers I and III would tend to unite Canadians if all Canadians adopted this type of nationalism. After all, civic nationalism encourages people of different ethnic, cultural, and linguistic backgrounds to harmoniously coexist. Speaker II's ethnic nationalism is a milder version of Speaker IV's ethnic nationalism. Speaker II does not seem to advocate separatism as Speaker IV does.

3. A

The foreign policy of the given nation is ultranationalistic. The nation pursues only its narrow nationalist interests and has no regard for the rights and freedoms of other nations. Such a foreign policy approach is represented by Position I on the spectrum.

Position II represents a nationalistic approach (an approach that gives priority to nationalistic goals but respects the rights of other nations), Position III represents a supranationalistic approach (limited support for the formation of international organizations), and Position IV represents an internationalistic approach (support for maximum cooperation between nations).

4. C

In the UN General Assembly, a voting group tends to contain like-minded member-states with common political, economic, and cultural goals.

The given criteria are not used by governments when making decisions about humanitarian aid (which is provided to suffering humans regardless of their ideology or culture) or locations for international conferences. By definition, national governments do not belong to nongovernmental organizations (NGOs); therefore, they cannot make membership decisions for NGOs.

5. A

The term *economic nationalism* refers to an economic policy of protectionism (the policy of imposing tariffs and quotas to restrict the inflow of imports and to protect domestic industries from foreign competition). Negotiating a free trade agreement with other nations would open up a nation to increased foreign competition; this would be inconsistent with a policy of economic nationalism.

All of the other strategies are examples of actions favoured by economic nationalists.

6. D

Quebec separatists believe the Québécois (Quebecers who speak French and are descended from the original settlers of New France) are a distinct nation. These separatists are seeking self-determination (the right of a nation to govern itself) for the Québécois.

Quebec separatism is motivated primarily by the desire for national self-determination (national independence), not by containment (the desire to prevent the expansion of the influence of a hostile nation or ideology), appeasement (the tendency to give into the demands of an aggressor in the attempt to prevent a war), or brinkmanship (pursuing a dangerous course to the brink of catastrophe in the pursuit of national goals).

7. A

Candidate I approaches the question from the most narrow (selfish) nationalistic perspective. This candidate, unlike the other three candidates, expresses no concern for people in human rights-abusing countries. Candidate I only cares about the economic prosperity of his or her own nation.

Candidate II is concerned about the benefits that international trade provides to people in other nations. Candidate III does not want to trade with any countries who commit human rights abuses. Candidate IV wants to use international trade to pressure other countries to improve their human rights records.

8. C

Candidate III proposes that nations that respect human rights should not trade with nations that violate human rights. This is the approach advocated by Amnesty International, a nongovernment agency devoted to protecting the rights of political prisoners ("prisoners of conscience") throughout the global community.

Amnesty International would not support the positions held by candidates I or II. Only as a second choice would Amnesty International support Candidate IV's position.

9. C

Nationalists worry that supranationalism (cooperation between nations through the formation of international organizations and/or the passing of international laws) threatens their economic and cultural sovereignty (independence). There is some truth to this, as membership in a supranational organization (such as the European Union) involves a nation's surrendering at least some independent control of its political, economic, and/or cultural affairs.

European nationalists rarely, if ever, oppose membership in the EU on the basis of international trade positions, citizens' rights and freedoms, or government funding of social problems.

10. C

The North American Free Trade Agreement (NAFTA) is a free trade agreement among Canada, Mexico, and the United States. It is an attempt at economic cooperation through closer trade links.

Nationalization (the government takeover of private industries) is not a goal of NAFTA. NAFTA's primary goal is regional economic cooperation (on the North American continent), not global economic competition.

11. C

An internationalist would support Canadian foreign policies that maintain Canada's involvement in international affairs. Therefore, an internationalist would support international alliances such as NATO, NORAD, and other free trade agreements, as well as Canada's involvement in peacekeeping and the international promotion of human rights.

An internationalist would answer *no* to questions I, V, and VII.

12. A

NAFTA (the North American Free Trade Agreement) is Canada's free trade deal with Mexico and the United States. The European Union (EU) is the world's largest free trade zone. Therefore, a report evaluating the pros and cons of the EU and NAFTA would be most relevant to question VI ("Should Canada pursue more free trade agreements with other nations?").

The other sources of information are not relevant to the issue of free trade.

13. A

The candidate seems to have favoured a foreign policy shift toward increased isolationism (non-participation in international agreements and non-involvement in international affairs). He wanted to dissolve NAFTA and stop foreign aid efforts.

The candidate did not recommend increased emphasis on global human rights protection. As an isolationist, he would have opposed increased American involvement in settling international disputes and American participation in global collective security operations.

14. A

The name *European Union* reflects the purpose of the union. What began as a free-trade zone in the 1950s has grown into an organization with aspirations of becoming a great power both economically and politically. Interestingly, the number of stars on the flag is incorrect. The European Union has, as yet, not increased the number of stars on the flag to reflect its recently increased membership. In terms of numbers of countries and people involved, the European Union is the largest free-trade zone in the world.

The goal of the European Union is to promote international cooperation between member nations, not to isolate them. Recently, the European Union has taken a more aggressive foreign policy stance; however, its main purpose is economic, not military. The European Union is basically a regional organization concerned with the issues of western Europe. It has no aspirations to replace the United Nations as a global organization.

15. B

It would be in the interest of any potential antagonist to consider diplomacy rather than engage in a war that neither might win and that would be costly to all parties involved.

Preventive diplomacy is not concerned with the attention of the media. Focusing the interest of the world community on an impending conflict might make a potential aggressor hesitate. Superpower involvement might deter potential antagonists from engaging in aggressive action. Preventive diplomacy usually involves international negotiations.

16. D

Internationalists try to improve the general welfare of the human race—not just that of individual nations. Since more spending on foreign assistance projects would improve conditions for many of the world's poor, this is what an internationalist would favour.

An internationalist would react negatively toward withdrawing from the WTO and reducing immigration, as both of these would reduce Canada's cooperation with other nations and/or make life difficult for many human begins. The purchase of long-range bombers would not be supported by internationalists because he or she would believe that offensive weapons such as these would endanger world peace.

17. A

The poster has two purposes: to raise funds for the war effort (through the sale of war bonds and stamps) and to maintain citizen morale (by stirring up national pride by showing a powerful American fist punching through the flag of Nazi Germany).

No details from the poster suggest that its purposes were to promote improve race relations, express concern about the financial costs of war, encourage pacifism, stop the United States from entering the Second World War, provide information about victories, or force the Germans to surrender.

18. C

At the end of the First World War, various nationalities demanded and obtained self-determination (a nation's right to determine its own government and handle its own affairs); for example, independent nation-states were created for Hungarians, Poles, Finns, Latvians, Lithuanians, and Estonians.

The creation of new nation-states at the end of the First World War was not motivated by the belief that the spread of democracy could threaten traditional European beliefs, that competition among nations would reduce the probability of future war, or that a second major European war would occur within 20 years.

19. A

The writer indicates the German invasion of Prague was not supported by the Czech people. For example, he notes that Czechs had to be forced to salute the invading Nazi soldiers because they would not do so willingly.

The writer does not suggest that other European nations approved of the German invasion of Czechoslovakia, that the invasion prevented an attack upon German territory, or that the Czechs violently resisted the Nazi invaders.

20. D

The 1939 German invasion of Prague was the result of Great Britain's attempt to appease Hitler at the Munich Conference in 1938. To avoid war with Germany, British prime minister Neville Chamberlain gave in to Hitler's demands for a piece of Czechoslovakia—the Sudetenland. Hitler rightly believed that Britain would not go to war over the rest of Czechoslovakia either, so he invaded it a few months after the Munich Agreement.

The 1939 invasion of Czechoslovakia cannot be interpreted to be the result of a British foreign policy of détente (an easing of tensions between hostile nations), isolationism (non-participation in international affairs), or containment (blocking an enemy nation from expanding its territory or further spreading its ideology).

21. **D**

The Japanese expanded their empire between 1931 and 1942 in order to gain control of raw materials that were not found in Japan.

Japan did not expand its territory to restore peace in Asia, prevent Western nations from establishing colonies in Asia, or liberate Asians from dictatorial rule.

22. **C**

Taken together, the two sources support the idea that citizens may suffer serious consequences when their nation chooses to act aggressively. The ultimate results of Japan's aggressive and imperialist foreign policy were the defeat of Japan, millions of Japanese casualties, and the destruction of Japanese cities (such as Hiroshima).

No details in the sources support the generalizations that wars are often started by nations seeking revenge for past defeats, that warfare in the 20th century was more humane than warfare in earlier times, or that differing military methods may be used to liberate ethnic groups living under the control of foreign rulers.

23. **A**

Amnesty International is a nongovernmental organization that campaigns for the human rights of prisoners of conscience (persons imprisoned merely because of their political or religious beliefs).

Amnesty International does not concern itself with environmental, foreign policy, or trade issues.

24. **D**

Some Canadians believe that continued trade with China will allow Canadians to develop a closer relationship with the Chinese people and then introduce the Chinese to democratic ideas and values through that relationship.

China's human rights record is much worse than that of Canada. Canadian human rights activists would, obviously, see human rights issues as important—probably at least as important as economic issues. Human rights activists would not justify trading with China—human rights activist would be concerned about improving rights in all countries.

25. **D**

The formation of the European Union in 1993 was the result of a series of actions that began in 1950 with an agreement between France and Germany to share control of their coal and steel industries. The agreement grew into the European Economic Community, or "Common Market." After the Second World War, there was a strong desire in Europe to avoid another war. Many people thought better trade relations (and greater interdependence) would be the best way to avoid another war. In time, the Common Market became the European Union.

Therefore, the European Union originated out of a desire to develop better trade relations between the Member States.

European states formed the Common Market to reduce trade barriers between Member States. They did not want to eliminate the political boundaries in Europe and join together in one state. Each country wished to increase trade and economic cooperation without surrendering its statehood. Britain and France were the only members of the Common Market that had nuclear weapons. Given that NATO had already been formed to protect Western Europe from a Soviet attack, there was no reason to create another European defensive alliance with nuclear capabilities. The goals of the Common Market were economic, not military. Improving environmental conditions in Europe was never a priority of the Common Market; the main goals of the Common Market were to promote greater economic prosperity in Western Europe through increased trade between Member States. This remains true of the European Union.

26. A

The National Energy Program (NEP) of 1980 to 1984 was an initiative of Pierre

Trudeau's Liberal government. The NEP increased federal taxes on Canadian petroleum resources—most of which were then found in the western provinces of Alberta and Saskatchewan. This took billions of dollars of oil-generated wealth out of Western Canada, which the federal government then used to lower oil and gas prices in other regions of Canada. Under the NEP, the federal share of oil tax revenues increased from 10 to 26 per cent, while Alberta's share declined to 37 per cent. Most Albertans saw the plan as another example of colonial exploitation of the West by Central Canada. The NEP definitely fuelled western alienation (western hostility toward the federal government and Central Canada) during the 1980s.

Multiculturalism was actually a very popular policy in the West, which is one of the most multicultural regions of Canada. Dissatisfaction with Canada's immigration policy has never been a cause of western alienation. Although the western provinces experienced massive cutbacks in education and health care during the 1980s and 1990s, this tended to increase resentment toward the provincial governments of the West (which were making the cutbacks), not hostility toward the federal government (which is not responsible for health and education).

27. C

The passage is taken from David Kilgour's book *Inside Outer Canada*. It identifies regional disparity as a major cause of regionalism and disunity in Canada.

The passage does not recognize regional diversity, misleading statistics, or equalization programs as causes of Canadian national disunity.

28. B

A *plural society* is a civil society in which several cultural groups coexist in a single territory, interacting in a peaceful way. All four speakers praise Canada for being such a society. In a plural society, the various groups ultimately become socially, politically, and economically dependent on one another.

Speaker IV praises Canada's federal system—but the other three speakers do not. All four speakers praise Canada for being more than a multiracial country. They praise the country for treating the various racial groups (and various other linguistic and cultural groups) in a tolerant way; that is, in the way that a plural society does. Although Speaker I mentions biculturalism, it is obvious that he and the other speakers admire more about Canada than its biculturalism (recognition and acceptance of Canada's British and French heritages).

29. B

All four speakers would probably support the encouragement of civic nationalism—a form of nationalism that is not based on the sharing of a common language, ancestry, race, ethnicity, or culture. What unites people in a civic nation is respect for the same laws, belief in tolerance, respect for minority rights, support for a democratic system of government, and a shared belief in liberal-democratic political ideals. The terms *civic nation* and *plural society* are synonymous.

The speakers are opposed to bigotry (prejudice and intolerance), cultural uniformity (eliminating cultural diversity), and ethnic segregation (keeping different cultural groups isolated from one another).

30. B

The term *social* refers to society (the customs and class structure of an ordered community). Statement II suggests that dissatisfaction with France's class structure (the division of society into three Estates) was a major cause of the French Revolution.

Statement I mentions a political cause of the revolution. Statement III refers to an economic cause of the revolution. Statement IV deals with an intellectual cause of the French Revolution.

31. C

The term *economic* refers to the production and distribution of wealth, the use of resources, and the government's management of the economy. Statement III mentions the economic troubles of France during the last days of absolutism.

None of the other statements mentions an economic cause of the French Revolution.

32. B

Speaker II states Italy's objectives in the First World War. Italy wanted to acquire ethnic-Italian territories within the Austro-Hungarian Empire. It also wanted to expand its empire by gaining control over foreign lands in the Balkans and in Africa.

Speaker I states Russia's foreign policy goals. Speaker III puts forward France's objectives in the war. Speaker IV states Britain's objectives in the First World War.

33. C

Speaker III represents France, whose foreign policy after the First World War focussed on the punishment of Germany. The speaker refers to recapturing Alsace and Lorraine, which were lost to Germany during the Franco-Prussian War, and imposing strict punishments on Germany to prevent it from being strong enough to threaten France's national security.

Speaker I describes Russia's aspirations for more territory, Speaker II describes Italy's desire to gain territory from Austria that it believes rightly belongs to Italy, and Speaker IV describes Britain's goal of preventing German dominance in Europe.

34. B

Image I is a propaganda poster that was designed to convince Soviet citizens to go along with Stalin's collectivization of agriculture. In other words, it was intended to encourage public support for agricultural reforms in the Soviet Union, specifically for the creation of collective farms.

The poster does not focus on private businesses or foreign investment. The poster was designed to bolster support for the nationalization (government takeover) of privately owned farms. Under Stalin's scheme of collectivization, lands were seized by the government and no compensation was paid to landowners.

35. C

Image I shows an idealized version of collectivization that suggests that the creation of collective farms had enriched the Soviet Union. In stark contrast, Image II shows the suffering that actually resulted from collectivization and other initiatives of Stalin's first Five Year Plan. Rather than hand over their livestock, grain, farm machinery, and farm buildings to the government, many Soviet peasants destroyed their possessions. Compounding the problem was the fact that Stalin was exporting the already scarce grain to finance the industrialization of the Soviet Union. To make matters even worse, Stalin purposely used starvation as a weapon to crush peasant resistance to collectivization. For example, in a government-created artificial famine in the Ukraine in 1932–33, millions of Ukrainian peasants were allowed to perish so that Stalin's power would increase and collectivization would take root.

Both images depict rural scenes; therefore, the sources do not show a contrast between urban lifestyles (lifestyles in towns and cities) and rural lifestyles (lifestyles in small farming villages). Both images are from the Stalinist era (1928 to 1953), so they are not contrasting life in Stalin's Soviet Union with life in Tsarist (pre-February 1917) Russia. Since the theme of both images is collectivization, the images cannot be interpreted as contrasting viewpoints on the industrialization of the Soviet Union.

36. C

National self-determination is the ability of a nation to govern itself without outside influence. The nation is usually comprised of people sharing a similar history, language, culture, or tradition.

None of the other definitions accurately define national self-determination.

37. D

The cartoonist suggests that Canada is reluctant to recognize the independence of Kosovo because it could create a "slippery slope" toward the resurgence of support for Quebec sovereignty.

The cartoon does not suggest that Stephen Harper was involved in the Kosovo independence movement, that the events leading the Kosovo's independence are the same as in Quebec, or that the state of Stephen Harper's career is dependent on the Quebec question.

38. B

In each of the given examples, genocide took place as a result of ultranationalism: the Holocaust in Germany, the famine in the Ukraine, and civil war between the extremist Hutus and Tutsis in Rwanda.

None of the other titles could be used to complete the given diagram.

39. C

During the war of independence in Kosovo from 1996 to 1999, war crimes including genocide took place against ethnic Albanians by Serb nationalists who were trying to prevent Kosovo from becoming independent.

None of the other named places experienced genocide as a result of ultranationalism during the dates given.

40. C

The Bloc Québécois is a federal political party whose main agenda is Quebec sovereignty. This group does not promote Canada's national identity.

The CBC, the RCMP, and Canada's peacekeepers are all institutions that promote various aspects of Canada's national identity.

41. C

The CRTC (Canadian Radio-television and Telecommunications Commission) is responsible for regulating the amount of Canadian content in all forms of media to ensure that Canadians are exposed to Canadian talent, information, and entertainment.

The CRTC does not regulate foreign investment, establish Canada's foreign policies, or provide security to Canada's political leaders.

42. C

The document presented by Jean Chrétien in 1969 that would have repealed the Indian Act and led the way for First Nations assimilation was called the "White Paper."

None of the other names listed are correct.

43. C

The National Indian Brotherhood was an organization that worked to promote the issues and concerns facing First Nations people in Canada. This group was instrumental in bringing down Chrétien's "White Paper" in 1969.

The Assembly of First Nations did not exist in 1969, as it is the successor to the National Indian Brotherhood. Neither the First Nations Confederacy nor the Congress of Aboriginal Peoples was instrumental in the defeat of the "White Paper."

44. B

Together with Robert Baldwin, Louis-Hippolyte Lafontaine worked to establish responsible government (elected representatives are accountable to Parliament and citizens for their decisions and policies) in Canada.

Louis-Hippolyte Lafontaine did not pass the BNA Act, lead the Métis rebellion, or establish French and English as official languages in Canada.

45. D

Patriotic nationalism is the expression of love for one's country, which is often expressed through feelings of loyalty. A willingness to die in combat is an example of this type of nationalism.

Situation I gives an example of linguistic nationalism. Situation II gives an example of cultural nationalism. Situation III gives an example of political nationalism.

46. C

Political nationalism occurs when people of a nation feel a sense of connectedness between them as a result of a shared desire for national self-determination and/or self-governance.

Situation I gives an example of linguistic nationalism. Situation II gives an example of cultural nationalism. Situation IV gives an example of patriotic nationalism.

47. B

Reconciling between two nationalist loyalties allows for a person to express nationalism for one country without sacrificing feelings of nationalism for another. By participating in Heritage Days, the immigrant is celebrating Canada's multiculturalism while also celebrating and promoting his or her country of origin.

None of the other situations gives an example of reconciliation between two nationalistic loyalties.

48. A

A *nation-state* is an independent country that has its own government and system of laws.

None of the other definitions provided accurately describe the term *nation-state*.

49. B

Bill 101 made French the official language of Quebec. It was very controversial because, although it was popular with Francophones, English-speaking Quebecers resented the legislation and large portions of the international community condemned it.

None of the other alternatives represents an example of conflict between Québécois and Canadian nationalism.

PRACTICE TEST 2

Use the following information to answer the next question.

In 1997, representatives of over one hundred nations met in Ottawa and signed an agreement to end the production and use of landmines.

1. The actions of these nations reflect an attempt to promote the values associated with

A. nationalism and militarism

B. isolationism and individualism

C. protectionism and egalitarianism

D. humanitarianism and internationalism

2. The **primary** role of the United Nations Security Council is to

A. decide questions involving international law

B. coordinate the daily work of United Nations' agency staff

C. create and oversee United Nations' peacekeeping operations

D. provide a public forum for debate among all member nations

3. Since the late 1980s, Canadian military personnel have **primarily** been involved in

A. maintaining a military blockade around Cuba

B. supervising Soviet troop withdrawals from eastern Europe

C. fulfilling Canada's NATO commitments in western Europe

D. supporting United Nations' peacekeeping and humanitarian efforts

Use the following information to answer the next two questions.

> I think it is a great idea for the nations of Europe to be united and to cooperate with each other. My country, Britain, shares many of the economic and political goals that are held by the other nations of Europe. However, the British government must also act to preserve British traditions and pride, and to keep a large degree of control over British political and economic affairs.
>
> —A British high school student

4. The student's comment provides support for Britain's membership in the

A. NATO Alliance

B. European Union

C. World Trade Organization

D. United Nations General Assembly

5. Which of the following statements **best** summarizes the position of the student?

A. Nations must balance international cooperation with national interests.

B. Strict rules must be placed on governments in order for nations to work together.

C. International cooperation only benefits nations suffering from economic hardship.

D. Conditions in the current global economy make it necessary for nations to join regional organizations.

6. The **main** reason Canada has joined free trade agreements is to achieve

A. global peace

B. national security

C. economic prosperity

D. international prestige

7. The League of Nations was designed to preserve peace **primarily** through

A. armed conflict

B. collective security

C. nuclear deterrence

D. military brinkmanship

8. The construction of the Maginot Line in the 1930s revealed France's belief that

   A. Germany remained a potential aggressor
   B. the United States would not remain a neutral nation
   C. the League of Nations could preserve peace in Europe
   D. Great Britain was seeking an alliance with the Soviet Union

Use the following information to answer the next two questions.

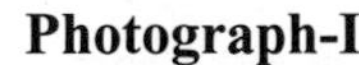

Photograph-I

Photograph-II

—from *Our World Today*

9. Taken together, the photographs could **best** be used in a report on the topic of methods used to

   A. create global economic equality
   B. resolve disputes between groups
   C. ensure protection of human rights
   D. encourage democratic political reforms

10. Which of the following generalizations is **most clearly** supported by the details of the two photographs?

A. Superpower nations continue to dominate the international political scene.

B. International terrorist organizations continue to be a threat to global security.

C. Nations may choose to form military alliances or remain neutral and non-aligned.

D. Disagreement among groups may be settled with violence or through negotiations.

11. Federal equalization payments are an instrument used to ensure that

A. regional diversity does not exist in Canada

B. all Canadian citizens are economically equal

C. provinces do not borrow money and accumulate deficits

D. the quality of health care and other services does not vary greatly from province to province

12. The Meech Lake Accord and the Charlottetown Accord were both unsuccessful attempts to

A. abolish Canada's Senate

B. amend Canada's Constitution

C. centralize political power in Canada

D. provide sovereignty association for Quebec

Use the following information to answer the next three questions.

Statement I

We are fed up with a federalism which classes the Quebec nation among the ethnic minorities in Canada. … With the help of the entire population, we want to replace this society of slaves with a free society. … Long live Free Quebec! Long live our comrades, the political prisoners! Long live the Quebec Revolution!

Statement II

It is more important to maintain law and order than to worry about those whose knees tremble at the sight of the army. … I think the society must take every means at its disposal to defend itself against the emergence of a parallel power which defies the elected power in this country.

Statement III

We are not prepared to use the preservation of law and order as a smoke-screen to destroy the liberties and freedom of the people of Canada... The Government is using a sledgehammer to crack a peanut. … We cannot protect democratic freedom by restricting, limiting and destroying democratic freedom.

Statement IV

It was, perhaps, the final irony in this Canadian drama. Two men had been kidnapped. The French Canadian lay dead. The Englishman went free.

—from *Columbo's Canadian Quotations*

13. All four of the given statements are related to the event known as the

A. October Crisis

B. Quiet Revolution

C. Northwest Rebellion

D. Conscription Crisis of 1917

14. The "sledgehammer" mentioned in Statement III is

A. Quebec's Bill 101

B. Lord Durham's report

C. the War Measures Act

D. General Middleton's forces

15. The "peanut" referred to in Statement III is the

A. FLQ

B. Métis

C. Parti Québécois

D. Quiet Revolution

16. Which of the following aspects of the British–German arms race caused the **most** tension between Britain and Germany during the 1905 to 1914 era?

A. The race to build aircrafts

B. The race to build warships

C. The race to manufacture artillery pieces

D. The race to manufacture machines guns

17. During the First World War, the opposing alliances were the

A. Axis and the Allies

B. Triple Entente and the Triple Alliance

C. Dual Alliance and the Entente Cordiale

D. Three Emperors' League and the League of Nations

Use the following information to answer the next question.

The federal government neither acted unilaterally nor destroyed the consensus when it patriated the Constitution and entrenched the Charter of Rights and Freedoms in 1982. True, the government of Quebec chose not to formally agree to the package. But it was a government of separatists who, despite all sorts of offers and concessions, were never interested in building a better Canada. Instead of wanting to improve the federal pact, they wanted to destroy it. So they were the ones who rejected the consensus on which it rested—not the majority of French-speaking Canadians, not the other provinces, and certainly not Ottawa.

18. The views of which of the following people on the *Constitution Act, 1982*, are expressed in the given quotation?

A. Pierre Trudeau

B. René Lévesque

C. Jacques Parizeau

D. Lucien Bouchard

19. During the 1920s and most of the 1930s, with regard to European affairs, the United States followed a foreign policy of

A. militarism

B. imperialism

C. isolationism

D. internationalism

Use the following information to answer the next question.

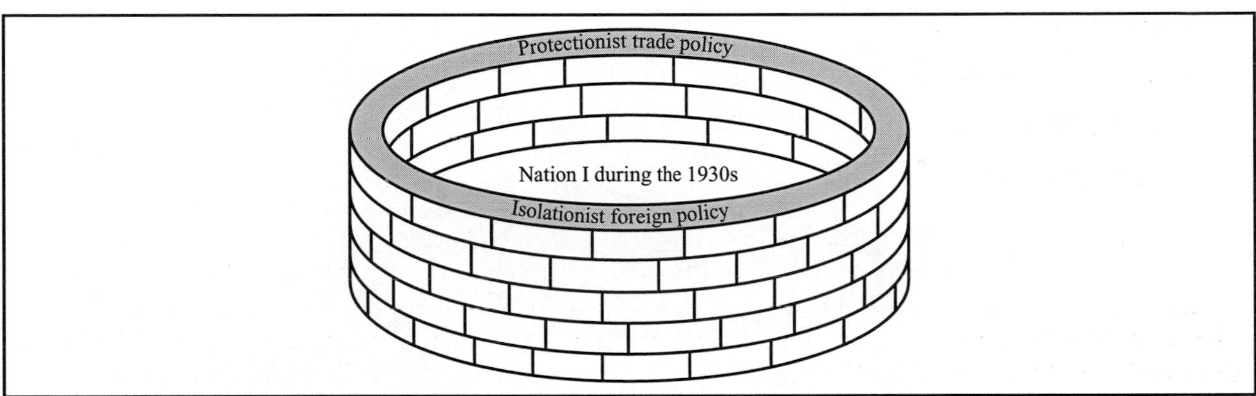

20. In the given diagram, Nation I represents

A. Spain

B. Canada

C. Great Britain

D. the United States

21. Which nation attempted to preserve its security by ensuring that Germany demilitarized the Rhineland and by building fortifications called the Maginot Line?

A. France

B. Poland

C. Czechoslovakia

D. The Soviet Union

22. In the early 1930s, the Nazi party in Germany made campaign promises that, if elected, it would

A. speed up the payment of war debts
B. use force to crush fascist movements
C. improve relations with France and Belgium
D. revive the economy and restore national pride

Use the following information to answer the next question.

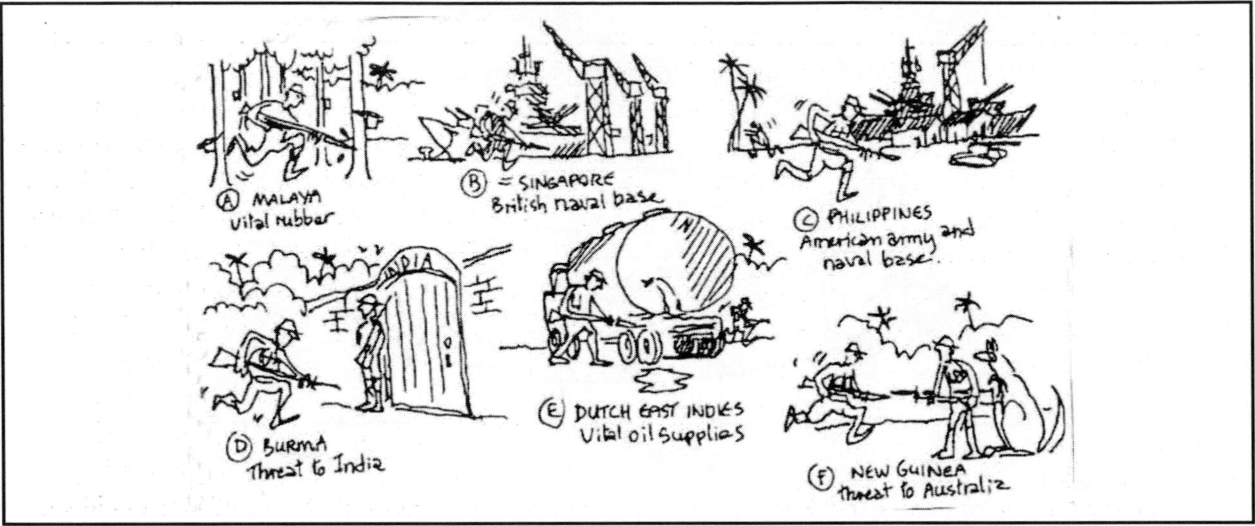

23. The given illustration suggests that Japanese aggression during the Second World War was **primarily** motivated by the

A. desire to spread Japanese culture throughout Southeast Asia
B. need to gain essential raw materials and strategic advantage
C. desire to free Asians from Western imperial domination
D. need to defend Japan from impending invasion

Use the following information to answer the next two questions.

EDITORIAL

In defence of Neville Chamberlain and appeasement

Many historians associate Neville Chamberlain and his use of appeasement with failure. It is time to rethink this judgement. It is time to speak in defence of appeasement. In the late 1930s, when Hitler made territorial demands beyond Germany's borders, few national leaders were willing to stand up to his demands. The role of chief negotiator fell to Neville Chamberlain, the British prime minister. The British people had witnessed the destruction caused by the First World War and feared the consequences for their country and Europe if another war broke out. Chamberlain knew that Germany had been treated harshly in 1919, perhaps too harshly, and that this treatment had caused great resentment, anger, and bitterness among the German people. Chamberlain was expected to negotiate with the ultimate representative of German hostility—Adolf Hitler. As Hitler made increasing demands for territory, Chamberlain, representing the British people, felt he had no choice but to "appease" Hitler to prevent war. The only alternative seemed to be an immediate confrontation that would lead to a war that Germany appeared better prepared to fight, and that most British citizens wanted to avoid at all costs. Chamberlain used his best diplomatic skills to negotiate and buy time for Britain to re-arm and prepare for war, but hoped that war could be avoided. Unfortunately, war was not avoided, only delayed until Hitler put into effect his plans for Nazi expansion. Chamberlain cannot be blamed for his reasonable and honest diplomatic attempts. He was, after all, negotiating with a dishonest and unreasonable dictator. Chamberlain was faithfully representing the wishes of the people who had elected him. Perhaps he was an idealist for believing that peace could best be accomplished by conducting calm and rational negotiations, but he should not be faulted for that. His efforts and ideals should be applauded, not condemned. Since 1945, it has become more obvious that maintaining world peace requires the willingness to compromise. To settle differences, there must be give and take between potential enemies. Appeasement should not be viewed as one of history's great failures. It should be viewed once again as a model of diplomacy that leaders and nations can use to stop aggression and avoid war.

24. The editor suggests the **most important** reason Chamberlain followed a policy of appeasement was to

A. create a buffer zone between Britain and the Soviet Union

B. avoid the devastation of a major international conflict

C. prevent Germany from expanding its territory

D. satisfy the demands of Britain's allies

25. Which of the following phrases from the editorial **best** explains the reason that appeasement failed to prevent the Second World War?

A. "few national leaders were willing to stand up to his demands"

B. "The only alternative seemed to be an immediate confrontation"

C. "Chamberlain used his best diplomatic skills to negotiate"

D. "He was, after all, negotiating with a dishonest and unreasonable dictator"

Use the following information to answer the next question.

We live in an era with a need greater than ever for coordinated, global political action and responsibility.

26. The writer of the given observation is calling upon governments to support greater

A. internationalism and collective security

B. regionalism and trade agreements

C. isolationism and self-interest

D. nationalism and sovereignty

27. Which of the following international organizations is paired correctly with its main purpose?

	Organization	Main purpose
A.	NORAD	Protect human rights
B.	NATO	Create a free trade zone
C.	European Union	Promote ethnic nationalism
D.	United Nations	Maintain international security

Use the following information to answer the next four questions.

Types of Nationalism
Type I
Shared among people who believe in similar ideas about law, values, and political traditions
Type II
Shared among people who feel a love for their country
Type III
Shared among people with similar traditions, artistic expressions, and food
Type IV
Shared among people who wish for self-determination for their nation

28. Which of the given types of nationalism **best** describes civic nationalism?

A. Type I

B. Type II

C. Type III

D. Type IV

29. Cultural nationalism is **best** described by

A. Type I

B. Type II

C. Type III

D. Type IV

30. A feeling of linguistic nationalism would **most likely** be shared by those who also share

A. Type I

B. Type II

C. Type III

D. Type IV

31. The type of nationalism **most strongly** encouraged by governments during times of war is

A. Type I

B. Type II

C. Type III

D. Type IV

Use the following information to answer the next question.

Group I	Cree people in Canada
Group II	Québécois in Canada
Group III	Inuit people in Canada
Group IV	Métis people in Canada

32. Which of the following statements is **true** for all of the given groups?

A. Each group considers themselves a nation-state within Canada.

B. Each group considers themselves a nation within Canada.

C. Each group is opposed to self-determination.

D. Each group desires separation from Canada.

33. Which of the following factors had the **least** influence in the shaping of nationalistic feelings leading up to the French Revolution?

A. Geographic

B. Economic

C. Political

D. Social

34. Which of the following countries has experienced the **most** conflicts among its inhabitants as a result of nationalism shaped heavily by geographic factors?

A. Israel

B. France

C. Canada

D. Great Britain

Use the following information to answer the next question.

Source I

"Youth gangs set fire to dozens of vehicles, fired on police and pelted a commuter train with rocks in the seventh straight night of violence in poor Paris suburbs.
Police poured into 10 Parisian suburbs but were unable to stop youths from setting more than 300 vehicles and two buses on fire. Nine people were injured overnight."

Source II

An angry mob of French citizens stormed the Bastille prison, releasing the prisoners held inside and murdering the governor and several prison guards. Sources suggest the mob was comprised primarily of peasants.

35. In both sources, the non-nationalistic loyalties that led to violence was related to

A. class

B. region

C. culture

D. religion

36. In an effort to keep the German race free from what the Nazis perceived to be inferiority and sub-human quality, the Nazi party

A. began the policy of lebensraum

B. established ghettos in the cities

C. passed the Nuremberg Laws

D. initiated Kristallnacht

Use the following information to answer the next two questions.

Definition I	Hitler's plan to eliminate the Jewish population in Europe
Definition II	Hitler's desire to secure land he believed Germany was entitled to
Definition III	A Nazi-sponsored raid on Jewish people
Definition IV	Slum areas in cities into which Jewish people were forced to live

37. Which of the given definitions correctly describes the term *lebensraum*?

A. Definition I

B. Definition II

C. Definition III

D. Definition IV

38. Which of the given definitions could also include the term *genocide*?

A. Definition I

B. Definition II

C. Definition III

D. Definition IV

39. The Soviet policy that led to the famine and the starvation of millions of Ukrainians from 1932 to 1933 was **primarily** rooted in the belief that

A. the Soviet Union and Stalin would gain international prestige as an economic powerhouse by producing the most grain of any country in the world

B. the only way for the Soviet Union to compete in the international economy was to make every bit of grain harvested available for sale

C. the citizens of the Ukraine had other resources for food and would not feel the effects of such stringent quotas for grain production

D. nationalistic tendencies in the Ukraine were a threat to the central power of the Soviet Union and needed to be eliminated

40. Which of the following continents has experienced much strife as a result of decolonization?

A. North America

B. Oceania

C. Europe

D. Africa

41. An example of a situation in which Inuit self-government was achieved was the establishment of

A. Nunavut

B. the reserve system

C. the Métis Settlements Accord

D. the Assembly of First Nations

42. Which of the following policies would **most likely** be adopted by a government with a commitment to internationalism?

A. Introduce tariffs on foreign goods and services

B. Establish quotas for foreign investment within the country

C. Participate in multinational economic summits and agreements

D. Provide subsidies to domestic businesses and industries that face fierce competition on the international market

43. Some people say the impact of Canada's involvement in organizations such as NAFTA negatively affects Canada by requiring some sacrifice of

A. sovereignty

B. multiculturalism

C. human rights record

D. commitment to internationalism

44. Which of the following stereotypes has had an impact on the development of a national identity among Canadians?

A. Canadians love hockey.

B. Canadians are not patriotic.

C. Canada is an aggressive nation.

D. Canada does not influence world affairs.

45. The former prime minister who was a federalist and who took a hard stand against the separatist movement was

A. Louis Riel

B. Pierre Trudeau

C. Sir Clifford Sifton

D. Louis-Hippolyte Lafontaine

46. One of the earliest leaders in Canada who worked to promote the inclusion of both French and English was

A. Louis Riel

B. Pierre Trudeau

C. Sir Clifford Sifton

D. Louis-Hippolyte Lafontaine

Use the following information to answer the next three questions.

Four Descriptions of Canadian Society

Description I

A society in which there are many different religious, ethnic, and cultural groups that are tolerated and accepted, and that have an impact on the administration of the country

Description II

A society in which people of many religious, ethnic, and cultural groups come together to develop ideas of Canadian identity and what it is to be Canadian

Description III

A country with a central government that has various religious, ethnic, and cultural groups of minorities who are able to govern themselves to a certain extent in order to preserve their uniqueness

Description IV

A country that works closely with its neighbours in economic, social, and ideological areas to ensure the promotion and development of each country

47. Which of the given descriptions describes a pluralistic view of Canada?

- **A.** Description I
- **B.** Description II
- **C.** Description III
- **D.** Description IV

48. A supporter of NAFTA would **most likely** agree with which of the given descriptions as an appropriate model for Canada?

- **A.** Description I
- **B.** Description II
- **C.** Description III
- **D.** Description IV

49. Which of the given descriptions would **most likely** be supported by a Québécois nationalist and a First Nations leader?

- **A.** Description I
- **B.** Description II
- **C.** Description III
- **D.** Description IV

ANSWERS AND SOLUTIONS—PRACTICE TEST 2

1. D	11. D	21. A	31. B	41. A
2. C	12. B	22. D	32. B	42. C
3. D	13. A	23. B	33. A	43. A
4. B	14. C	24. B	34. A	44. A
5. A	15. A	25. D	35. A	45. B
6. C	16. B	26. A	36. C	46. D
7. B	17. B	27. D	37. B	47. A
8. A	18. A	28. A	38. A	48. D
9. B	19. C	29. C	39. D	49. C
10. D	20. D	30. C	40. D	

1. **D**

The landmine treaty is founded upon humanitarianism (a concern for the welfare of all human beings, regardless of their nationality) and internationalism (a belief that nations should cooperate on matters of common concern or common interest). The main purpose of the landmine treaty is to relieve the pain and suffering of ordinary human beings who continue to be killed or maimed by landmines long after wars have ended.

The signing of the landmine treaty was not based on the values associated with nationalism (concern only for the narrow interests of one's own nation), militarism (eagerness to go to war), isolationism (non-participation in world affairs), individualism (concern only for one's own rights, not the rights of larger groups), or protectionism (support for trade barriers between nations).

2. **C**

The primary role of the UN Security Council is to initiate and supervise United Nations' peacekeeping operations.

It is the role of the International Court of Justice, not the Security Council, to decide questions of international law. The UN Secretariat coordinates the daily work of UN staff. The UN General Assembly provides a forum for debate among all UN member states.

3. **D**

With the exception of the first Gulf War in 1990 to 1991, the Canadian military's role has mainly been in the area of humanitarian and peacekeeping efforts under the banner of the United Nations.

Only American warships were involved in the military blockade of Cuba, and this incident occurred during the Cuban Missile Crisis of 1962. The withdrawal of Soviet troops from eastern Europe has largely been left up to those countries where Soviet troops were stationed, such as Poland and Czechoslovakia. Since the end of the Cold War, Canada has steadily reduced its military presence in western Europe.

4. B

Since the student's comment refers to Britain's involvement with other nations of Europe that have similar economic and political goals, he is providing support for Britain's membership in the European Union. The EU is a supranational organization of European countries committed to economic and political cooperation through integration.

NATO is primarily a military alliance. The student is showing support for economic and political—not military—cooperation. The World Trade Organization and the United Nations General Assembly include countries from all regions of the world. The student is showing support for a union of European nations only.

5. A

The student's position advocates Britain's involvement in a union of European nations, but not to the point at which Britain would completely lose its political and economic sovereignty (its power to independently make important economic and political decisions). Thus, it supports the idea that nations must balance international cooperation with their own national interests.

While the student wants some conditions to be imposed on his country's involvement in the international community, he does not call for strict rules and he favours considerable freedom of action for his nation. There is no evidence in the student's statement to support the conclusions in alternatives C or D.

6. C

Free trade agreements are designed to improve the economic prosperity of the countries who participate.

Free trade agreements are not primarily designed to promote global peace, national security, or international prestige, even though these may result.

7. B

The League of Nations was designed to preserve peace primarily through collective security (mutual defence against aggression). According to the principle of collective security, whenever one member of the League was attacked, all other members were obliged to defend it.

The League did not plan on forcing peace on the world with armed conflict or military brinkmanship (using the threat of war to achieve goals). Nuclear weapons were not developed until 1945, so the League (1920–1946) could not have hoped to prevent wars with the threat of nuclear retaliation.

8. A

The Maginot Line was built along the border between France and Germany. The Maginot Line was a string of massive fortifications intended to make France secure from a German attack.

If the French had feared that the Americans would one day become an enemy, they would have built an ocean fleet instead of a wall (since the Atlantic Ocean lies between France and the United States). Because France believed the United States would remain neutral in a future European war, France felt that constructing the wall was necessary. France did not have much faith in the ability of the League of Nations to provide collective security against aggression. Neither Britain nor France wanted an alliance with the Soviet Union until late in the 1930s, after the Maginot Line was built. Also, Britain and France were allies and relied on each other, and France did not feel threatened by Britain.

9. B

Photographs I and II show two very different activities—war and diplomacy. Both war and diplomacy are methods of resolving disputes between groups. The soldiers in Photograph I are at war. The Security Council members in Photograph II are practicing diplomacy (conducting negotiations). Peace and security are the main concerns of the Security Council. Discussing methods of achieving or maintaining peace is probably what the delegates are doing in Photograph II.

No details in the photographs suggest that they represent methods used to create global economic equality or indicate the people shown are protecting human rights. The photographs cannot be interpreted with certainty as representations of methods used to encourage democratic political reforms.

10. D

Disagreement among groups may be settled with violence or through negotiations. When groups of people have serious disagreements, they can fight (Photograph I) or they can talk out their problems (Photograph II).

Photograph II could support the generalization that superpower nations continue to dominate the international political scene because the United States and Russia have had more influence than most countries in the Security Council since it was formed in 1945. However, the picture of two soldiers in an unidentified war (Photograph I) does not support this generalization. Neither photograph supports the generalization that international terrorist organizations continue to be a threat to global security. Photograph I suggests the two men depicted are soldiers—not terrorists—fighting in a modern war.

The Security Council does concern itself with international terrorism on occasion, but nothing in Photograph II indicates that this is one of those occasions. No details in either photograph specifically support the generalization that nations may choose to form military alliances or remain neutral and non-aligned.

11. D

Federal equalization payments attempt to make sure that great differences in the quality of health care, education, and other services do not exist among Canada's provinces and territories.

Equalization payments are not an attempt to create total economic equality among the citizens of Canada. They are simply an attempt to make provinces more comparable in essential services. They do not restrict a province's ability to borrow money or accumulate deficits. They are not an attempt to eliminate regional diversity.

12. B

The Meech Lake Accord (1990) and Charlottetown Accord (1992) were unsuccessful attempts to change (amend) Canada's Constitution. Their primary goal was to accommodate Quebec, which had refused to approve the 1982 Constitutional deal brokered by Pierre Trudeau.

Neither accord attempted to abolish the Senate (although the Charlottetown Accord sought to reform it) or to award Quebec sovereignty association (national independence for Quebec, but with close economic ties to the rest of Canada). Both accords sought to decentralize the Canadian federation (grant more power to the provinces) rather than to centralize the federation (concentrate more power in the hands of the federal government).

13. A

All four statements relate to the October Crisis. Statement I is from the FLQ Manifesto, Statement II was made by Prime Minister Trudeau during the October Crisis, Statement III is from NDP leader Tommy Douglas, and Statement IV from Brian Moore's 1971 book *The Revolution Script*.

The four statements do not refer to the Quiet Revolution, the Northwest Rebellion, or the Conscription Crisis of 1917.

14. C

The "sledgehammer" refers to the War Measures Act, which was invoked during peacetime for the first and only time in October 1970.

NDP leader Tommy Douglas was not referring to either Quebec's Bill 101, Lord Durham's report, or General Middleton's forces in his 1970 response to the proclamation of the War Measures Act.

15. A

The "peanut" hammered by the War Measures Act "sledgehammer" was the Front de libération du Québec (FLQ). It was a terrorist organization that used force and terror in an unsuccessful attempt to separate Quebec from Canada.

NDP leader Tommy Douglas was not referring to the Métis, the Parti Québécois, or the Quiet Revolution in his 1970 response to the proclamation of the War Measures Act.

16. B

Although Britain and Germany raced to produce all kinds of armaments in the years before the First World War, no aspect of this arms race caused more tension between the two powers than the race to build warships. By 1900, Britain had been the world's dominant naval power for more than a century; the British wanted to maintain this dominance of the seas for reasons of national security, economic security, and national pride. As an island country with a large overseas empire, Britain felt most threatened by Germany's naval buildup. Britain understood that a naval blockade of the British Isles could easily bring down the empire. Britain also understood that military supremacy at sea was the only way to counteract German military supremacy on land. The British assumed that Germany desired a large navy to wrestle away colonies from more established empires and/or to achieve European and global domination.

The race to build aircrafts, manufacture artillery pieces, and manufacture machine guns did not cause more tension than the race to build warships.

17. B

During the First World War, the two opposing alliances were the Triple Alliance (Germany, Austria-Hungary, and Italy) and the Triple Entente (Britain, France, and Russia).

The Axis and the Allies were the two opposing alliances in the Second World War. The Dual Alliance and Entente Cordiale were earlier alliances that had evolved into the Triple Alliance and Triple Entente by 1914. The Three Emperors' League was the 1873 to 1887 alliance between Germany, Austria, and Russia.

18. A

The given quotation is an excerpt from *The Essential Trudeau.* In it, Trudeau suggests Quebecers had no real reason to resent the way the Constitution was patriated in 1982.

The three Québécois separatist leaders—Lévesque, Parizeau, and Bouchard—saw Trudeau's patriation of the Constitution as a betrayal of Quebec, which had refused to support the patriation process, the new Constitutional amending formula, or the 1982 Charter of Rights and Freedoms.

19. C

During the years from 1919 to 1941, the main foreign policy approach of the United States was isolationism (non-involvement in the affairs of foreign nations).

The United States did not adopt the foreign policies of militarism (military buildup), imperialism (the building of an empire), or internationalism (extensive cooperation with other nations).

20. D

The United States attempted to isolate itself both politically and economically from the rest of the world during the interwar period in the hope that it would not be drawn into future world conflict.

During the 1930s, Spain was wracked by a brutal civil war between Fascists and anti-Fascists, but it cannot be said to have adopted isolationist or protectionist policies. During the 1930s, Canada made several trade agreements with other members of the British Commonwealth. Although Canada was not strongly involved in international affairs, it could not be said to be isolationist. Britain was heavily involved in international affairs in the 1930s.

21. A

France ensured that Germany demilitarized the Rhineland and France constructed the Maginot Line along its border with Germany.

None of the other nations took these steps to ensure their security.

22. D

The Treaty of Versailles left Germany in a weakened military and economic state. Hitler promised the Germans that his Nazi party would revive the economy and restore national pride, in part by ignoring the terms of the Treaty.

Hitler had no intention of recognizing the terms of the Treaty of Versailles that required Germany to pay war reparations. Hitler's Nazi party was a fascist movement. It was unlikely he would advocate the crushing of such movements. Rather than advocate improved relations with France and Belgium, the Nazi party attempted to arouse national pride against these countries, which had made Germany pay economically crippling war reparations after the First World War.

23. B

The given illustration depicts the raw materials (natural resources) and strategic importance of each country.

There is no mention of the desire on the part of the Japanese to spread their culture throughout Asia, the desire to free Asia from Western imperialism, or any threat against Japan by other countries.

24. B

There are numerous references in the editorial to Chamberlain's desires to avert war.

The Soviet Union is not even mentioned in the editorial. The editorial indicates that Chamberlain was perfectly willing to allow German territorial expansion up to a point. There is no reference to Britain's allies in the editorial.

25. D

The fact that Hitler was quite willing to lie and break any promise he made inevitably led to disillusionment with appeasement and the beginning of the Second World War.

Appeasement, in part, is the willingness to back down in the face of threats or aggression. This phrase "few national leaders were willing to stand up to his demands" simply states the idea of appeasement in a different way. An immediate confrontation would (in Chamberlain's view) have led to war. Chamberlain was a skilled diplomat and negotiator.

26. A

The writer's statement calls for coordinated global (worldwide) action. This implies support for the foreign policy approaches of internationalism (dedication to the general welfare of the human race) and collective security (a global defence partnership against aggression).

The writer calls for support for global (worldwide) action. He wants nations to concern themselves with the welfare of the world community, not just with their own regional or national interests.

27. D

One of the main goals of the United Nations is to maintain world peace through collective security.

NORAD (North American Aerospace Defence Command) is a military alliance; it is not a human rights protection organization. NATO (North Atlantic Treaty Organization) is a military alliance; it is not a free trade agreement. The European Union is an organization that strives for the economic and political integration of Europe by promoting international cooperation and a multicultural European civic nationalism. Promoting ethnic nationalism (a force that tends to divide Europeans rather than unite them) is certainly not the main goal of the EU.

28. A

Civic nationalism binds people together through a shared belief in the same laws, values, and political traditions. This is described by Type I.

Type II best describes patriotic nationalism. Type III best describes cultural nationalism. Type IV best describes political nationalism.

29. C

Type III describes cultural nationalism, which is when a group of people share a common culture with similar traditions associated with food, attire, or artistic expressions.

Type I best describes civic nationalism. Type II best describes patriotic nationalism. Type IV best describes political nationalism.

30. C

Type III describes cultural nationalism, which is when a group of people share a common culture with similar traditions associated with food, attire, or artistic expressions. Linguistic nationalism is shared among people who share the same language, which is closely linked to culture.

Type I best describes civic nationalism, Type II best describes patriotic nationalism, and Type IV best describes political nationalism. None of these would be as closely linked to linguistic nationalism as would cultural nationalism.

31. B

Type II describes patriotic nationalism, which is the love for one's country, and it is this type of loyalty that governments attempt to encourage among their citizens in order to gain support for a war. It is also this type of nationalism that people feel when they are prepared to sacrifice their lifestyles or even lives in the name of their country.

Type I best describes civic nationalism. Type III best describes cultural nationalism. Type IV best describes political nationalism. None of these types are usually as important to governments during times of war as is patriotic nationalism.

32. B

Each of the given groups is a distinct cultural group that considers itself a nation within Canada.

A nation-state implies the groups consider themselves to be sovereign countries, which is not the belief these groups hold about themselves. The groups do not desire separation from Canada, and each group is in favour of self-determination.

33. A

Geography played the smallest role in shaping nationalistic feelings in France, as loyalty to the land was not a major feeling during that time.

Economic, political, and social factors all played a large role in the influence of nationalistic feelings among the French population.

34. A

Much of the conflict that has erupted in Israel has been caused by the fact that various cultural groups feel a strong sense of nationalism to the land on which the country is situated. People of Jewish, Islamic, and Christian faiths each claim ownership of the land, and as result there has been fighting over control of the area.

None of the other nations listed has experienced the violence that Israel has as a result of nationalism tied to geography.

35. A

Both sources point out that the violence was a result of anger among people of lower classes in society (the poor).

None of the other loyalties is at issue in either of the sources.

36. C

The Laws for the Protection of German Blood and German Honor (part of the Nuremberg Laws) forbade marriage and sexual relations between Jewish people and non-Jewish people because the Nazis believed Jews to be inferior and they wanted to prevent the mixing of races within German society.

Lebensraum was the belief that the German people needed "living space" and should take over areas, such as Austria and Czechoslovakia, to get it. Kristallnacht was a Nazi-sponsored raid on Jewish people across Germany. The establishment of ghettos allowed the Nazis to control the movement of Jewish people in Germany and other countries under Nazi control.

37. B

***Lebensraum* means "living space," and it expressed Hitler's desire to take over areas such as those in Austria and Czechoslovakia that he believed rightly belonged in Germany.**

Definition I correctly describes Hitler's Final Solution. Definition III correctly describes Kristallnacht (Crystal Night or Night of Broken Glass). Definition IV describes the Jewish ghettos.

38. A

Genocide is the elimination or attempted elimination of an entire race of people. Hitler's Final Solution, his attempt to eliminate the Jewish population, is considered to be an example of genocide.

Definition II describes *lebensraum*, but Hitler's attempt to take over countries is not in itself considered genocide. Kristallnacht, as described by Definition III, and the ghettos, as described by Definition IV, were tools used by Hitler to subjugate and isolate the Jewish population but not to eliminate them.

39. D

Feelings of nationalism were growing in the Ukraine in the years leading up to the famine. This was a threat to Moscow, as the Ukraine was a major source of income for the Soviet government. It was believed the famine manufactured by Soviet policies would prevent these feelings from growing because people would be starving and unable and/or unwilling to pursue these nationalist ideas.

Although international competition and prestige were reasons leading to the Soviet policies, they were not at the root of the implementation of the policies leading to the famine. The goal of the policies leading to the famine was widespread hunger and poverty—the Soviet government did not want the Ukrainian people to have a source of sustenance.

40. D

The continent of Africa was colonized during the Age of Imperialism, primarily by European countries. Since decolonization, many African countries have experienced civil war and many atrocities as various groups attempt to take control since the departure of the colonist countries.

None of the other areas experienced the same type of colonization, and therefore none has experienced the strife that Africa has as a result of decolonization.

41. A

The establishment of Nunavut was the largest land claims settlement in Canadian history and gave a form of self-government to the Inuit people of Canada's North.

The reserve system was not applied to the Inuit people. The Métis Settlements Accord applies only to the Métis people. The Assembly of First Nations is a lobby group that works on behalf of Canada's First Nations peoples.

42. C

Internationalism is a belief in cooperation in order to promote the common good for all countries. By participating in multinational economic summits and agreements, the government would be demonstrating a commitment to working with other countries in terms of the economy.

The introduction of tariffs, provision of subsidies to domestic businesses, and setting of quotas for foreign investment are all policies that contradict internationalism and promote protectionism in the economy.

43. A

Canada's membership in organizations such as NAFTA (North American Free Trade Agreement) means that it works with other countries to achieve common economic goals. However, critics of these types of agreements suggest that in order to placate the demands of other members, some of Canada's sovereignty must be sacrificed.

Neither Canada's multiculturalism nor human rights records are said to be sacrificed by critics of such agreements. Membership in an organization such as NAFTA demonstrates a commitment to internationalism.

44. A

Hockey has become a part of the Canadian identity through stories of success, and it is an integral part of Canadian childhood. Although there are many Canadians who are not hockey fans and who have never played hockey, the sport has gained an iconic status within the country. Canadians often identify themselves with hockey, and many people from around the world view Canada as a "hockey nation."

That Canada has an aggressive nature is not a view held by many Canadians. Generally, Canadians believe themselves to be patriotic but prefer to demonstrate patriotism in a subdued manner. Canada's influence in world affairs has had little, if any, impact on the development of an identity among Canadians.

45. B

Pierre Trudeau was prime minister of Canada, and he was a federalist, which means he believed that Quebec should remain part of Canada. He took a hard stand against the separatist movement, especially during the FLQ Crisis of 1970.

Louis Riel was instrumental in the establishment of Manitoba as a province, as well as being the leader of the Métis during the Northwest Resistance of 1885. Sir Clifford Sifton was most known for his belief that Canada needed to establish aggressive immigration policies in order to populate the country. He was also known for his defence of the western part of the country and the issues unique to the region. Louis-Hippolyte Lafontaine was the prime minister of the United Province of Canada (the union of Upper and Lower Canada). He wanted to include both French and English in the establishment of the country and was against the violence that broke out between the two groups.

46. D

Louis-Hippolyte Lafontaine was the prime minister of the United Province of Canada (the union of Upper and Lower Canada). He wanted to include both French and English in the establishment of the country and was against the violence that broke out between the two groups.

Louis Riel was instrumental in the establishment of Manitoba as a province, as well as being the leader of the Métis during the Northwest Resistance of 1885. Sir Clifford Sifton was most known for his belief that Canada needed to establish aggressive immigration policies in order to populate the country. He was also known for his defence of the western part of the country and the issues unique to the region. Pierre Trudeau was prime minister of Canada, and he was a federalist, which means he believed Quebec should remain part of Canada. He took a hard stand against the separatist movement, especially during the FLQ Crisis of 1970.

47. A

Pluralism is the belief in the importance of varied cultures, each having an impact on the country without being segregated from each other.

Pluralism does not suggest that people should have the same ideas about identity or that minority groups should have self-government. Description IV suggests geographical integration with other countries, which is not part of pluralism.

48. D

Description IV describes geographical integration, which is a goal of NAFTA (North American Free Trade Agreement) in which the economies of Canada, the United States, and Mexico are integrated.

Descriptions I, II, and III suggest models of Canada that have priorities that are likely not as important for a supporter of NAFTA.

49. C

Both Québécois nationalists and First Nations leaders would likely support a society in which minorities are granted self-governance, as both of these groups are currently seeking such status in Canada.

Pluralism (description I), assimilation (description II), and geographic integration (description IV) would not likely be supported by a Québécois nationalist or First Nations leader.

Appendices

GLOSSARY

Aboriginal	First Nation, Métis, and Inuit peoples
Aboriginal self-determination	A vision that many Aboriginal groups hope to see realized in Canada; in this vision, Aboriginal groups would have the power to form a type of self-government that would give them control over issues affecting the everyday lives of Aboriginal peoples
Arctic Council	A forum consisting of eight member countries as well as permanent participants representing groups of indigenous peoples living in the Arctic
civic nationalism	Nationalism that binds people together through a shared belief in the same laws, values, and political traditions
cultural nationalism	Nationalism that brings together a group of people who share a common culture with similar traditions, artistic expressions, foods, and attire
ethnic nationalism	Nationalism that brings together people who share a common ethnic history, usually with generations of ancestors sharing that ethnicity
European Union	A community of 27 European nations; the EU works to promote peace and economic stability among members
Fathers of Confederation	Leaders of the colonies that participated in the conferences that led to the creation of the British North America Act, which made Canada a country in 1867
First Nations treaties	Agreements made both before and after Confederation between the Canadian government and First Nations people
French Canadian nationalism	A feeling of nationhood among Francophones in Canada who wish to preserve the French language and culture in Canada
General Assembly	A main body within the United Nations that meets to discuss issues of worldwide importance, ranging from economic, to humanitarian, to social, to environmental
genocide	The intentional elimination of a group of people based on race, religion, ethnicity, or other cultural factors
identity	A condition in which people feel a sense of similarity or sameness with others of their religion, race, ethnicity, or nationality
internationalism	The belief in the importance of cooperation among countries in order to promote the common good for all countries in both social and economic terms
l'Organisation internationale de la Francophonie	An organization of 55 countries and 13 observers in which the French language is prevalent and part of the country's or observer's history
legitimacy	A return to monarch control with little concern for the nationalistic feelings of the citizens

linguistic nationalism	Nationalism that exists among people who share a similar language and a desire to protect it even if they are of different ethnicities or cultures
multination model	In this model, government systems are organized to allow a minority group to have a form of self-government and form a majority in a specific area within the confines of a larger nation
nation	A group of people with similar cultures, traditions, and languages who inhabit a specific area but do not have the ability to govern themselves and do not possess characteristics of a nation-state.
National Indian Brotherhood	An organization formed in 1968 to represented Status and Treaty Aboriginal groups in Canada; in 1982, it re-formed into the Assembly of First Nations
nationalism	A feeling of pride in and devotion to one's country or nation
nation-state	A sovereign country in which the majority of its members often share common cultures, traditions, and languages
patriotic nationalism	Nationalism that exists when people have a shared feeling of love for their country
pluralistic society	Exists when there are people of many different cultural and ethnic groups living within a country
political nationalism	Nationalism that exists when people share a desire to govern themselves independently and without influence from other countries
pursuit of national interest	The effort made by a country to ensure that actions taken both domestically and internationally benefit the country as a whole
religious nationalism	Nationalism that exists when people share the same or similar religious beliefs
Security Council	A main body within the United Nations that decides if, when, and how the UN will become involved in conflict around the world
self-determination	The desire for a group of people with common culture, history, and language to have control over their own country.
spiritual nationalism	Nationalism that is related to both religion and a person's relationship to the land
ultranationalism	Exists when feelings of pride and devotion result in actions or policies that are detrimental to other nations and/or the citizens of that country
United Nations	An organization made up of 192 countries that works to promote peace and security around the world
World Council of Indigenous Peoples	An organization that existed from 1975 to 1996; it worked to promote the rights of indigenous peoples around the world

CREDITS

Some questions, preambles, and graphics appearing in this booklet have been reproduced from Social Studies Provincial Examinations, with the permission of Alberta Education. Every effort has been made to provide proper acknowledgment of the original sources and to comply with copyright law. However, some attempts to establish original copyright ownership may have been unsuccessful. If copyright ownership can be identified, please notify Castle Rock Research Corporation so that appropriate corrective action can be taken.

Some images in this document are from www.clipart.com, © 2013 Clipart.com, a division of Getty Images.

52 Quote by Josef Stalin. *From Russia and the USSR: 1905-56* by John Laver, Hodder and Stoughton Educational, 1997

57 From *Twentieth Century History: The World Since 1900* by Tony Howarth, Longman Group Ltd., 1979

"Five Scenarios for Separation" from *Review of International Affairs*, Belgrade. As found in "World Press Review," May 1991

59 From *Internationalism: Opposing Viewpoints Series* edited by Bruno Leone, Greenhaven Press, Inc., 1978

60 From *On This Day* edited by Sian Facer, Octopus Publishing Group Limited, 1992

86 From The Chicago Tribune as found in *A Cartoon History of United States* Foreign Policy Pharos Books, 1991, Chicago Tribune Company, All rights reserved

88 From "Global stability has its price" by Stephen Rosenfeld. published in *The Edmonton Journal*, (May 30, 1994) p. A8

137 From "The 20th Century, Second Edition" M.N. Duffy, Basil Blackwell Publisher, 1983

142 Excerpt from "Agenda for Peace" in *Canada and the World* (vol. 59, no. 1, 1993)

143 Poster from *Persuasive Images: Posters of War and Revolution*, by Peter Paret, Beth Irwin Lewis, and Paul Paret, copyright © 1992 Princeton University Press.

144 Article from *The Illustrated History of the 20th Century*, Dorling Kindersley Limited, London, 1997.

145 I Map from *World History in the Twentieth Century: New Edition* by R.D. Cornwell (Longman Group Ltd., 1969).

II -Photograph from *History of the Modern World: World War Two* by Robert Hoare (Macdonald Educational Ltd, 1973).

148 Excerpt from *Inside Outer Canada* by David Kilgour, Lone Pine Publishing, Edmonton, 1990

152 I Poster from *Persuasive Images: Posters of War and Revolution*, by Peter Paret, Beth Irwin Lewis, and Paul Paret, copyright © 1992 Princeton University Press.

II Photograph from: http://www.infoukes.com/history/famine/gregorovich/index.

154 Cartoon "Stephen Harper on slippery slope with Kosovo Independence" as published in *The Edmonton Journal* (Feb. 19, 2008) p. A14

156 From Government to unveil Indian Act changes CBCNews.ca, June 14, 2002, http://www.cbc.ca/canada/story/2002/06/14/firstnations_bill020614.html

162 I-Photograph from *Chronicle of 20th Century Conflict* by Neil Grant (Reed International Books Limited, 1993).

II-Photograph from *Our World Today* by Derek Heater (Oxford University Press, 1985).

164 From *Colombo's Canadian Quotations* edited by John Robert Colombo, Hurtig Publishers, 1974

I Excerpt from FLQ Manifesto, October 8. 1970

II Pierre Trudeau, from interview with TV Reporter Tim Rolfe, October 13, 1970

III Tommy Douglas, from speech to the House of Commons, October 16, 1970

167 Illustration from *Our World this Century* Derek Heater, Oxford University Press, 1982

172 From Paris suburbs hit with more violence CBCNews.ca, November 3, 2005 http://www.cbc.ca/world/story/2005/11/03/paris-riot051103.html

ORDERING INFORMATION

SCHOOL ORDERS

Schools and school jurisdictions are eligible for our educational discount rate. Contact Castle Rock Research for more information.

***THE KEY* Study Guides** are specifically designed to assist students in preparing for unit tests, final exams, and provincial examinations.

***THE KEY* Study Guides**—$29.95 each plus G.S.T.

SENIOR HIGH		JUNIOR HIGH	ELEMENTARY
Biology 30	Biology 20	English Language Arts 9	English Language Arts 6
Chemistry 30	Chemistry 20	Mathematics 9	Mathematics 6
English 30-1	English 20-1	Science 9	Science 6
English 30-2	Mathematics 20-1	Social Studies 9	Social Studies 6
Mathematics 30-1	Physics 20	Mathematics 8	Mathematics 4
Mathematics 30-2	Social Studies 20-1	Mathematics 7	English Language Arts 3
Physics 30	English 10-1		Mathematics 3
Social Studies 30-1	Mathematics 10 Combined		
Social Studies 30-2	Science 10		
	Social Studies 10-1		

Student Notes and Problems (SNAP) Workbooks contain complete explanations of curriculum concepts, examples, and exercise questions.

SNAP Workbooks—$29.95 each plus G.S.T.

SENIOR HIGH		JUNIOR HIGH	ELEMENTARY
Biology 30	Biology 20	Mathematics 9	Mathematics 6
Chemistry 30	Chemistry 20	Science 9	Mathematics 5
Mathematics 30-1	Mathematics 20-1	Mathematics 8	Mathematics 4
Mathematics 30-2	Physics 20	Science 8	Mathematics 3
Mathematics 31	Mathematics 10 Combined	Mathematics 7	
Physics 30	Science 10	Science 7	

Class Notes and Problem Solved—$19.95 each plus G.S.T.

SENIOR HIGH		JUNIOR HIGH
Biology 30	Biology 20	Mathematics 9
Chemistry 30	Chemistry 20	Science 9
Mathematics 30-1	Mathematics 20-1	Mathematics 8
Mathematics 30-2	Physics 20	Science 8
Mathematics 31	Mathematics 10 Combined	Mathematics 7
Physics 30		Science 7

Visit our website for a tour of resource content and features or order resources online at
www.castlerockresearch.com/store/

#2410, 10180 – 101 Street NW
Edmonton, AB Canada T5J 3S4
e-mail: learn@castlerockresearch.com

Phone: 780.448.9619
Toll-free: 1.800.840.6224
Fax: 780.426.3917

ORDER FORM

THE KEY	QUANTITY
Biology 30	
Chemistry 30	
English 30-1	
English 30-2	
Mathematics 30-1	
Mathematics 30-2	
Physics 30	
Social Studies 30-1	
Social Studies 30-2	
Biology 20	
Chemistry 20	
English 20-1	
Mathematics 20-1	
Physics 20	
Social Studies 20-1	
English 10-1	
Math 10 Combined	
Science 10	
Social Studies 10-1	
Social Studies 9	
English Language Arts 9	
Mathematics 9	
Science 9	
Mathematics 8	
Mathematics 7	
English Language Arts 6	
Mathematics 6	
Science 6	
Social Studies 6	
Mathematics 4	
Mathematics 3	
English Language Arts 3	

Student Notes and Problems Workbooks	QUANTITY SNAP Workbooks	QUANTITY Solution Manuals
Mathematics 31		
Biology 30		
Chemistry 30		
Mathematics 30-1		
Mathematics 30-2		
Physics 30		
Biology 20		
Chemistry 20		
Mathematics 20-1		
Physics 20		
Mathematics 10 Combined		
Science 10		
Mathematics 9		
Science 9		
Mathematics 8		
Science 8		
Mathematics 7		
Science 7		
Mathematics 6		
Mathematics 5		
Mathematics 4		
Mathematics 3		

Problem Solved and Class Notes	QUANTITY Class Notes	QUANTITY Problem Solved
Mathematics 31		
Biology 30		
Chemistry 30		
Mathematics 30-1		
Mathematics 30-2		
Physics 30		
Biology 20		
Chemistry 20		
Mathematics 20-1		
Physics 20		
Mathematics 10 Combined		
Mathematics 9		
Science 9		
Mathematics 8		
Science 8		
Mathematics 7		
Science 7		

Total Cost

Subtotal 1	
Subtotal 2	
Subtotal 3	
Cost Subtotal	
Shipping and Handling*	
G.S.T	
Order Total	

*(Please call for current rates)

School Discounts

Schools and school jurisdictions are eligible for our educational discount rate. Contact Castle Rock Research for more information.

PAYMENT AND SHIPPING INFORMATION

Name:____________________

School Telephone:____________________

SHIP TO

School:____________________

Address:____________________

City:__________ Postal Code: ______

PAYMENT

□ By credit card VISA/MC

Number:____________________

Expiry Date: ____________________

Name on card: ____________________

□ Enclosed cheque

□ Invoice school P.O. number: ______

#2410, 10180 – 101 Street NW, Edmonton, AB T5J 3S4 **Phone:** 780.448.9619 **Fax:** 780.426.3917
Email: learn@castlerockresearch.com **Toll-free:** 1.800.840.6224
www.castlerockresearch.com

CASTLE ROCK RESEARCH CORP